THE EUROPEAN HISTORY SERIES

SERIES EDITOR

KEITH EUBANK

ARTHUR S. LINK
GENERAL EDITOR FOR HISTORY

DAUGHTERS OF REVOLUTION

A HISTORY OF WOMEN IN THE U.S.S.R.

BARBARA EVANS CLEMENTS

THE UNIVERSITY OF AKRON

HARLAN DAVIDSON, INC.

ARLINGTON HEIGHTS, ILLINOIS 60004

TO G. G. N.

Copyright © 1994
Harlan Davidson, Inc.
All Rights Reserved
This book, or parts thereof, must not be used or
reproduced in any manner without written permission.
For information, address the publisher, Harlan Davidson, Inc.,
3110 North Arlington Heights Road,
Arlington Heights, Illinois 60004-1592.

Library of Congress Cataloging-in-Publication Data
Clements, Barbara Evans, 1945–
Daughters of revolution: a history of women in the U.S.S.R. /
Barbara Evans Clements.
    p. cm. — (European history series)
    Includes bibliographical references and index.
    ISBN 0-88295-908-5
    1. Women—Soviet Union—Social conditions. 2. Women—Russia—Social
conditions. 3. Soviet Union—Social conditions. I. Title.
II. Series: European history series (Arlington Heights, Ill.)
HQ 1662.C57 1994
305.4'0947—dc20
                                                      93–29309
                                                      CIP

Illustration credits appear on p. 171
Cover illustration: Detail from a famous World War II Soviet poster
by I. M. Toidze, 1941. The poster reads *The Motherland is Calling.*

Manufactured in the United States of America
97 96 95 94 93 1 2 3 4 5 MG

FOREWORD

Now more than ever there is a need for books dealing with significant themes in European history, books offering fresh interpretations of events which continue to affect Europe and the world. The end of the Cold War has changed Europe, and to understand the changes, a knowledge of European history is vital. Although there is no shortage of newspaper stories and television reports about politics and life in Europe today, there is a need for interpretation of these developments as well as background information that neither television nor newspapers can provide. At the same time, scholarly interpretations of European history itself are changing.

A guide to understanding Europe begins with knowledge of its history. To understand European history is also to better understand much of the American past because many of America's deepest roots are in Europe. And in these days of increasingly global economic activity, more American men and women journey to Europe for business as well as personal travel. In both respects, knowledge of European history can deepen one's understanding, experience, and effectiveness.

The European History Series introduces readers to the excitement of European history through concise books about the great events, issues, and personalities of Europe's past. Here are accounts of the powerful political and religious movements which shaped European life in the past and which have influenced events in Europe today. Colorful stories of rogues and heroines, tyrants, rebels, fanatics, generals, statesmen, kings, queens, emperors, and ordinary people are contained in these concise studies of major themes and problems in European history.

Each volume in the series examines an issue, event, or era which posed a problem of interpretation for historians. The chosen topics are neither obscure nor narrow. These books are neither historiographical essays, nor substitutes for textbooks, nor monographs with endless numbers of footnotes. Much thought and care have been given to their writing style to avoid academic jargon and overspecialized focus. Authors of the European History Series have been selected not only for their recognized scholarship but also for their ability to write for the general reader. Using primary and secondary sources in their writing, these authors bring alive the great moments in European history rather than simply cram factual material into the pages of their books. The authors combine more in-depth interpretation than is found in the usual survey accounts with synthesis of the finest scholarly works, but, above all, they seek to write absorbing historical narrative.

Each volume contains a bibliographical essay which introduces readers to the most significant works dealing with their subject. These are works that are generally available in American public and college libraries. It is hoped that the bibliographical essays will enable readers to follow their interests in further reading about particular pieces of the fascinating European past described in this series.

Keith Eubank
Series Editor

CONTENTS

PREFACE

February 23, 1917, was a bright, sunny, almost springlike day in Petrograd, Russia's capital on the Gulf of Finland. Strikes and demonstrations against the government of Nicholas II—Emperor, Grand Duke of Finland, Tsar of all the Russias—began early that morning. By afternoon, crowds were swirling through the city, singing, yelling, waving banners, their spirits energized by the mixture of elation and apprehension that people often seem to feel when defying governments that are thrashing on the brink of collapse. It was a demonstration like many others, but with this difference: women started it. They started it that morning when they poured out of the factories where they worked to shout for food and an end to World War I. After two more weeks of continuous unrest in which women played an equally noisy part, on March 2, 1917, Nicholas abdicated, ending the Romanov dynasty that had ruled Russia for 300 years. Russians marvelled that women had started a revolution.

Seventy-four years later, in August 1991, another political confrontation brought women into the streets of the Russian capital. This time the city was Moscow, and the weather was dreary; the rain of late summer had come, mixed with the exhaust of ten thousand diesel engines, and now bathed the city in a dirty smog. Tanks were in the streets, ordered there by a faction of the governing Communist Party. What the troops were supposed to do was unclear, and as the young draftees of the Soviet army waited nervously for orders, crowds milled around them. Before them and behind them they found women—middle-aged ones in flowered dresses, older ones with headscarves firmly knotted under their chins—ordinary Soviet women. Many were there to harangue the soldiers in the time-honored Slavic way of mothers to their sons. "We are your mothers, your wives, your sisters," cried one in tears as she

cradled her dog in her arms. "Why do you want to shoot us?" The soldiers cringed in embarrassment; few could reply.[1]

Some blocks away there were other women—younger, slimmer, many in jeans—milling around in front of the White House, the tall, flat-faced building that was the seat of the Russian Federation Parliament and the headquarters of resistance to the coup. They stayed on the steps from midday Monday, August 19, when the troops entered Moscow, to late on Wednesday, August 21, when the announcement came that the leaders of the conspiracy had been arrested. Should the army storm the building, they and the young men, mostly students who had gathered there, intended to form a human wall. The crisis ended without an attack. The students celebrated. Once again a government had fallen in Russia, once again women had marched and shouted and pleaded and helped to push it over. But this time, people did not wonder that women had been involved. After all, women had built factories in the 1930s, they had dug trenches around Moscow as the bombs fell in the summer of 1941, they were doctors and lawyers and cosmonauts. Why should they not face down tanks?

For much had changed for women in the seventy-four years that lay between the February Revolution and the August coup. Monarchical, peasant Russia became the Union of Soviet Socialist Republics, a world power and industrial giant whose communist ideology was embraced by governments that ruled over more than half the peoples of the earth. Traditional village society gave way to modern cities in a helter-skelter process driven by a party apparatus that amassed enormous political power and committed equally enormous atrocities. Global war heaped on more difficulties. In all the momentous developments that marked this seventy-four-year history of the Union of Soviet Socialist Republics, women played an important part. And in doing so, they remade the way they lived in the society and the way the society responded to them.

---

1 This particular woman was observed by Jehanne Gheith of Stanford University. See Jehanne Gheith, "Impressions of a Coup: Moscow, August 1991," *Women East-West* (Newsletter of the Association for Women in Slavic Studies), November 1991, 10.

The history of women in the Soviet period—what they did and how the great changes in their world affected them—is the subject of this book. The contribution women made to Soviet society will be a major theme of this history. So too will be the Soviet experiment in women's emancipation, one of the most far-reaching any government has ever attempted. Understanding this history requires detailed consideration of the ways in which Soviet society defined "feminine" and "masculine" and how those definitions (which themselves changed over time) both affected social developments and were affected by them. Of course all the women of the many ethnic groups in the Soviet Union played their parts in this story, but particular attention must be paid to the Europeans—the Russians, Ukrainians, Belorussians, Jews, Lithuanians, Estonians, and Latvians. They made up the majority of the population, and their history, particularly that of the Russians and Ukrainians, affected the lives of all the others.

The study of women's history brings to the forefront topics that are not commonly given much attention in other historical fields. Sexuality, gender, social roles, patterns of family life, all these must be carefully analyzed in order to understand women's history. Women's history also asks students to look at well established historical issues in new ways. By studying the politically weak rather than the powerful, women's history provokes a reconsideration of how change occurs in societies. When is government leading, and when is it following public opinion? Do political revolutions actually change societies? What are the connections between revolutions and processes of far longer duration, such as industrialization?

All these questions arise when studying the history of women in the Soviet period of Russian history. To answer them, Russian history must be put in its European context, for the history of Soviet women can only be understood by beginning with the premise that the great majority of Soviet women belonged to a pan-European culture that rested on shared beliefs and very similar economic and political systems. Well into the nineteenth century most women all across Europe were peasants who lived in tightly knit village communities and got by on what they could grow or make themselves. The small minority of upper-class women managed estates and participated in the power struggles of an hereditary, landowning elite. The political values that pervaded this European world were patriarchal, that is, they gave power to men, particularly to older men. The Europeans believed that God had created women and the young physically and morally weaker than mature men, and had therefore intended them to be under men's control. Women owed men obedience and submission, men owed women protection and guidance.

Women responded to patriarchal values in very similar ways across the continent; that is, they accepted them as divinely ordained, and found consolation and hope in religion and also in the rewards they earned by performing their prescribed roles well. For rank and age had their prerogatives, too. Centuries of aristocratic political organization and eons of family-based social organization had made it possible for European women to derive status, privileges, and power from their age and social position: older women were entitled to respectful treatment from younger men; upper-class women were accustomed to ordering about all lower-class men.

There were variations from society to society in the severity of patriarchal norms, of course, and it is important to be attentive to the ways in which those variations affected the history of women in Russia and the U.S.S.R. Some notable differences arose out of Russia's history as an Orthodox Christian society. Historically, Russian culture laid great stress on subordination, submissiveness, and self-sacrifice for men as well as women. These values were nurtured particularly by the church and by Russia's political elite; they permeated all levels of the society and were expressed in the stories of lives of the saints as well as in rules for male-female relations within the family.

Even more significant was Russia's problematical relationship to the rest of Europe. Isolated by distance and often by hostile relations with the neighbors on its western borders, Russia was relatively untouched by the political, economic, and cultural stirrings that signalled the beginning of the Renaissance elsewhere on the continent as early as the twelfth century. Consequently, important changes in women's situation in Western Europe in the late Middle Ages such as rising rates of literacy and the emergence of the nuclear family did not come to Russia until centuries later. When they did come, they came very quickly and at government initiative. The forced pace of change set up an important dynamic of action-and-reaction, a tension between government and nation that often produced cycles in which the inrush of new ideas and initiatives was followed by a period of response that included both resistance and then eventual synthesis of innovation and tradition.

This dynamic shaped Russia's modernization and therefore the history of women in Russia. Modernization—the transformation of rural societies dependent on subsistence agriculture into urban societies chiefly dependent on industrial production—revolutionized women's lives all over Europe. It raised the standard of living, moved the population from the country to the towns, and promoted egalitarian political and social values. Assessing its impact involves paying particular attention to those elements most important for women. These include: (1) the movement of women into the public world of formal education, waged labor, and politics; (2) changes in women's familial roles; and (3) attendant changes in cultural definitions of woman's nature and of her position in society. There were many similarities here between the experience of Russian and other European women because of the culture they all shared and because the Russian modernizers deliberately copied Western European models. Equally significant, however, were the differences, some of them a legacy from Russia's past, others the consequence of the conditions and events of the Soviet period.

To understand the history of women in the U.S.S.R., all these elements must be considered—the inheritance of Russian history, the underpinnings of European culture, modernization in general and in its particular Russian-Soviet form, the course of events in the Soviet period, and finally, the enormous diversity of the Soviet peoples. It is necessary always to keep in mind the dangers of generalizing about all women, especially the women of a nation as huge and varied as the Soviet Union. The several generations of Soviet women shared a historical inheritance and made a history together, so it is meaningful to consider their experience as a whole. But millions of women from more than one hundred different ethnic groups, despite their many commonalities, differ from one another in myriad ways. Those differences will figure prominently from time to time in this book.

So too will the actions of influential women, who made important contributions to Soviet history. For the most part, however, the great patterns in the experience of Soviet women will largely occupy attention. Those who wish to understand the richness and complexity of Soviet women's history are urged to consider this book only the briefest of introductions.

Note on the Calendar and Transliteration

Until February 1918 Russia used the Julian calendar, which was twelve days behind the Western (Gregorian) calendar in the nineteenth century, and is thirteen days behind in the twentieth. In what follows here, Russian dates will be given.

Russian words and names will be transliterated according to the Library of Congress system, with these exceptions: (1) diacritical marks will be omitted; (2) some first names with close equivalents in English will be anglicized (Alexandra, not Aleksandra); (3) certain names well known in the West will be spelled according to the most common usage (Yeltsin, not Eltsin).

1 / THE LEGACY OF THE NINETEENTH CENTURY

The nineteenth century bequeathed to women in Russia an inheritance of ancient customs, mixed with new ideas and rapid changes. Throughout the century, tradition dominated the lives of aristocrats and peasants alike. By the third quarter of the nineteenth century, however, an urban world of technological marvels and difficult new problems rose to challenge tradition and to call centuries-old beliefs about women into question.

WOMEN IN TRADITIONAL SOCIETY

The Peasants

In the nineteenth century, peasant women of the Russian Empire spent most of their lives working, first in their parents' households, then in the households of the families they married into. On the plains of the Ukraine or Central Asia, in the forests of Siberia, in the mountains of the Caucasus, women grew vegetables, gathered wild foods, tended livestock, made clothing and handicrafts, carried water, harvested crops, preserved food, cooked, and cleaned. They also bore and nursed many babies. Russia was a poor country, where only the rich, a tiny proportion of the population, could escape lives of continual labor. In this subsistence economy, never far from the edge of hunger, the reward for hard work was survival.

Because they had to work together to feed themselves and pay their taxes to the nobility and government, the peasants of the Russian Empire, like peasants elsewhere, prized values that strengthened village solidarity. Thus they stressed the importance of cooperation and shared decision-making among the families that made up the community. But, thanks to other age-old traditions, they also subscribed to a stern patriarchalism that accorded tremendous power to the senior men of the village. The young were to obey the old; women were to obey men. God had revealed his intentions, the peasants believed, by making women inferior to men. Women who refused to kneel to male authority were subjected to punishments that ranged from public ridicule to severe beatings.

Life is rarely as tidy as religious doctrines and social codes say it should be, and the reality of village life in the traditional societies of the Russian Empire often fell short of the ideal of powerful patriarchs, dutiful wives, and submissive children. Families squabbled and broke apart, villagers hatched feuds with one another and then continued them for generations, wayward sons defied their fathers, and strong women henpecked weak men. Furthermore, the power of the patriarchs was limited by customs that permitted leeway for less powerful members of the community to express themselves. Festivals gave people the opportunity to let off steam. Among the Russians there was also a long-standing practice of young men leaving the village with their friends to seek work elsewhere and hence escape parental control temporarily. The law extended some limited protection to the weak. And peasant society granted women a sphere of their own, one within which they could achieve authority and status that men generally shied away from challenging.

This sheltered enclave emerged from the gender-based division of power and labor within the family and village. Among the Slavs, older women occupied a place in the family analogous to the supreme position enjoyed by their husbands; that is, they commanded the obedience of all junior women, primarily their daughters and daughters-in-law, and demanded the respect of their sons. The authority of such women was probably the source of the legend that Russian women were more powerful and domineering than women elsewhere in Europe. In fact the position of Russian peasant women was very similar to that of their counterparts in other countries, for it was common throughout Europe for women to wield considerable power within their own realm of activities. Older women customarily assigned work to younger ones and then supervised them as they performed their tasks. Older women were responsible for controlling the behavior of younger ones (and of young boys too) by teaching them morality and punishing their misbehavior. Naturally they took care of younger women as well, nursing them when they were sick and helping them in childbirth. They passed on to their daughters and granddaughters their knowledge of medicine, sex, agriculture, and cookery, their proverbs and lullabies, their family histories, tales of their ancestors, tips on the propitiation of evil forces, and legendary fragments of the Christian story.

Thus the patriarchy of the Russians and of the other European peoples of the Russian Empire, for all its severity, permitted, even encouraged women to develop their own hierarchy of relations, their own bonds of solidarity, and their own folklore. Peasant society also rewarded women for following the rules set down for them. Above all, older ones who had worked hard and reared healthy children could expect to carry weight in the family and to live out their lives in some security. This may help to explain why peasant women, though they often complained about the hardships of existence, ordinarily conformed no less than men did to their world and accepted much of it as arising from the natural order of things. It is just as well that they did. For until the great changes unleashed by modernization began to reach the villages, and even long afterwards, women had few alternatives.

The Nobility

Before the nineteenth century the majority of the noblewomen of the Russian Empire were ethnic Russians, women who, despite their high rank in society, had much in common with the peasant serfs they dominated and exploited.[1] Patriarchal values, as we noted earlier, extended to all the women of Russian society, enjoining aristocrats as well as peasants to submit to the authority of their menfolk. Noblewomen, like peasant women, stood in the wings of the male political stage. Excluded from holding or inheriting political office, they participated in elite politics only indirectly, through relationships with men. But aristocrats, like peasants, also practiced a division of labor and

---

1 Serfdom existed in Russia from the sixteenth century to 1861.

authority within the family that permitted a separate woman's world to flourish. Noblewomen passed on much the same folklore to their children as did peasants, and worshiped the same divinities in the same churches with them, looking at the same icons and listening to the same priestly chants and admonitions. Indeed, until the eighteenth century they also dressed in much the same way and spoke the same language.

Of course upper-class women lived more comfortable lives, for they enjoyed greater wealth and status. Noblewomen were subordinate to men, but only to those who held the same or higher social rank. They exercised considerable power over peasant men, particularly their own serfs. Naturally the work of noblewomen was also easier than that of the peasants, consisting largely of managing households and of light domestic tasks such as sewing.

Differences between peasants and nobles grew greater in the eighteenth century, after Peter the Great (1682–1725) launched the westernization of the Russian aristocracy. Peter, himself the son of an unusually well-educated noblewoman, Natalia Naryshkina, saw women's traditionalism as one of many clogs to national development and quite deliberately included among his programs the westernization of noblewomen as well as noblemen. Female courtiers, and later those less eminently placed, were encouraged to adopt Western styles of dress and deportment, and to learn their letters. The evidence suggests that Russian noblewomen embraced these changes enthusiastically. As the eighteenth century proceeded, therefore, their lives increasingly diverged from those of peasant women, with important consequences for both groups and for Russian history.

The Women of the Borderlands

Noble and peasant women of Slavic (primarily Russian and Ukrainian) ancestry made up the majority of women in Russia's traditional society. A middle class comprising Russians, Ukrainians, Belorussians, Jews, and Tatars was based in the cities and making its living in commerce; but until modernization began to transform the economy in the second half of the nineteenth century this mercantile class was very small, amounting to no more than 1 or 2 percent of the population. More significant to the general history of women in the U.S.S.R. were the many non-Russians living on the borderlands of the Empire.

By the end of the nineteenth century, more than one hundred distinct ethnic groups, or "nationalities" as the government called them, lived within the Russian Empire. They were an astonishingly diverse assortment of peoples. The inhabitants of the Caucasus and Central Asia were mostly of Turkic ancestry and Islamic faith, but they differed from one another in customs and in lifestyle, some being nomads who lived in tents and followed their flocks, others being merchants or farmers who had settled centuries before in villages or towns. The dense forests and forbidding tundra of Siberia were home to a variety of hunter-gatherer groups distantly related to the Native Americans, as well as to a motley population of free peasants, runaway serfs, merchants, convicts, and political prisoners from European Russia. On the Baltic coast lived Latvians, Estonians, Lithuanians, Germans, and Finns, Europeans with historic ties to the Poles and Germans. In religion most of these peoples were either Muslim or Christian, but some were animists who worshipped the forces of nature. Most, like the Slavs, lived in patriarchal societies, but there was considerable variation from group to group. While the Christian Armenians and Georgians professed most of the same patriarchal beliefs as the Russians, the peoples of the Pacific coast generally practiced a good deal of egalitarianism in the relations between the sexes. The Muslims—Azeris and other Caucasian peoples as well as Central Asians and the descendants of the Tatars (many of whom lived scattered through the communities of central Russia)—demanded female subordination in the greatest degree. Their practices included veiling, polygamy, and the sequestration of women in special parts of the household, but even among them there were significant differences, depending on the historic development of the individual groups and on whether they were sedentary or nomadic.

The Russian government had extended its control over these peoples through a process of conquest that took centuries. Central Asia, the last area to be subdued, did not finally submit to the Russian army until the 1880s. After takeover, the government usually made few efforts to change the customs of the conquered, being content to extract taxes from them and reward their leaders if they cooperated. The result was that a very small elite became Russified while the rest of the people continued to live in traditional patterns. In the nineteenth century, therefore, the non-European women of the borderlands, as well as those such as the Tatars, who lived interspersed within the Slavic population, remained largely unaffected by the changes that already were beginning to revolutionize the lives of many Russian as well as western and central European women.

WOMEN AND MODERNIZATION IN THE NINETEENTH CENTURY

By the middle of the nineteenth century the tsarist government had succeeded in westernizing the country's nobility. Russian courtiers were polished and sophisticated, at home in the capitals of Western Europe; Russian intellectuals were beginning to make their mark in European high culture. Less successful had been the government's efforts to reorganize itself, for it proved far more difficult to change bureaucrats' inefficient habits than it was to change the nobles' taste in clothes and ideas. Furthermore, by the middle of the nineteenth century, many government officials recognized that more sweeping reforms than any they had yet undertaken were necessary to make Russia into a great European power. Most important was the building of an industrialized economy, a formidable undertaking in social as well as economic engineering. Industrialization required skilled workers, industrious entrepreneurs, and educated professionals. Russia had few of these. In order to produce them, Tsar Alexander II (1855–1881) abolished serfdom in 1861 and thereafter promoted the expansion of education and economic development. His successors, Alexander III (1881–1894) and Nicholas II (1894–1917), presided over the beginnings of Russian industrialization. All these tsars soon found to their consternation, however, that the changes they had unleashed had consequences they had never intended. Among these were unexpected alterations in the lives of women, nobles and peasants alike.

Noblewomen

Throughout the nineteenth century, the majority of noblewomen still spent most of their days running their households and performing the multitude of arduous, time-consuming tasks that kept a family fed, clean, and warm in those days before electrical appliances and indoor plumbing. But the transformation initiated by tsarist governments did affect them. Over the course of the century, most noblewomen became literate. They got into the habit of reading magazines and novels, as well as prayer books and other religious writings. Many among the upper ranks of the aristocracy and within the intelligentsia (the intellectual and artistic sector of society, a group which, by the second half of the nineteenth century, included both aristocratic and middle-class elements) were becoming reasonably well educated. They studied foreign languages, literature, science, and mathematics (often with foreign-trained governesses and tutors), lived during the winters in lavish town houses in Moscow or St. Petersburg, and traveled often to Western Europe. Alexandra Kollontai, a future revolutionary, had a childhood that, superficially at least, was typical. Born in 1872, the daughter of a general of Ukrainian ancestry and a Finnish-Russian noblewoman, Kollontai grew up with her time divided between her family's estate in Finland and their large apartment in St. Petersburg. She was educated first by an English governess and later by tutors, and could speak five languages by the time she was ten. In truth, privileged children such as Kollontai had more in common with the aristocrats of Vienna or London than they did with the illiterate, overworked peasants of their own country.

A very extensive pattern of social and legal restrictions continued to affect the lives of noblewomen, however, even the richest. Women of all social ranks still entered marriages arranged by their families, they could not divorce if their marriages failed, and, whether married or single, they possessed few legal rights. Indeed, Russian law and custom placed liabilities on noblewomen that were not common elsewhere in Europe. Chief among these were those deriving from the suspicious tsarist government's internal passport system. All adult subjects of the

SOFIA PEROVSKAIA

Sofia Perovskaia was a much revered, much despised female revolutionary. The first woman publicly executed in Russia for political offenses, she went to her death in 1881 smiling contemptuously at the hangman. Her demeanor and the actions that had brought her to the gallows confounded many of the nineteenth century's ideas about femininity. Perovskaia was the daughter of an important general in the Russian Army, and yet she had led a terrorist organization that killed a king. Faced with death, she remained calm, refusing to beg for clemency. Conservative Russians saw her as a diabolical figure; revolutionaries considered her a martyr to the cause of liberating the poor.

The real Perovskaia was neither saint nor demon, but she was certainly an extraordinary woman. Born in 1853, she grew up in a home dominated by an autocratic father. Sofia sided with her submissive, devoutly religious mother, but learned to despise submission. In school in the late 1860s, she joined a group of politically radical young women who were studying socialism. Soon she came to believe that the authoritarianism of her father was only one manifestation of the tyranny that gripped all Russia. She then became a model socialist revolutionary—serious, stern, even humorless, as well as austere, selfless, and dedicated to the cause of change. She had a confidence in her own rightness, and a proud, somewhat withdrawn spirit that inspired others. Women were particularly impressed by Perovskaia's unwillingness to defer to her male comrades. In 1876 she was one of the founders of Land and Liberty, an illegal organization dedicated to teaching the peasants to rise up against the landlords and the government.

It was a hopeless task for a few hundred revolutionaries. By 1879 Perovskaia had become so frustrated by her political impotence that she turned to terrorism. If the revolutionaries assassinated tsarist officials, particularly the tsar himself, she argued, the peasants would see that their rulers were both incompetent and mortal, and would conclude that revolution could succeed. Then they would revolt. Acting on this naive assessment of Russian realities, she and her lover Andrei Zheliabov organized a new group called "The People's Will" that laid a series of traps for Alexander II over the next two years. He managed to elude them until March 1881. Perovskaia was not among those who actually killed the tsar, but she had made the plans that led to his death.

Her arrest, trial, and execution came quickly. Throughout she remained serene. She expressed no regret over the fact that the peasants not only failed to rise in revolution but simply continued to go about their daily work. Nor did she acknowledge that she had helped to bring an ardent conservative, Alexander III, to the throne. To the end she kept her feelings to herself, feeding the legend of the iron-willed noblewoman who courted martyrdom by committing murder.

tsar were required to register their residences as well as their travels with the police and to carry identity papers, commonly called passports. Rather than have their own passports, women were listed on the passports of male relatives, usually fathers or husbands. They thus had to acquire not only the government's permission but their relative's to travel or to move, and married women were prohibited by law from living apart from their husbands. In addition, although women at all levels of society could own property, they needed the consent of their husbands to manage it. Only widows and the very small number of single women in the upper class could attain any genuine legal and economic independence.

The Intelligentsia and the "Woman Question"

The laws governing women, and the subject of Russian patriarchalism generally, became central issues in a heated debate among educated subjects of the tsar that began in the 1850s and continued until the Revolution. The reform-minded intelligentsia was centered in Russia's major cities and composed primarily of people of European ethnicity. In the mid-nineteenth century, they came to see women's subordination to men as emblematic of the still larger and more pervasive injustice of Russia's patriarchal monarchy. The great Russian novelists Ivan Turgenev, Fedor Dostoyevskii, and Leo Tolstoy made the victimization of women by men an important theme in their novels. Women were praised for their suffering and self-sacrifice by poets such as Nikolai Nekrasov. And Nikolai Chernyshevskii, a well-known socialist of the 1860s, inspired several generations of young Russians with his novel *What Is to Be Done?* (1863), in which a young woman named Vera Pavlovna rebels against conventional society and dedicates herself instead to social reform. The oppressed woman became a central motif of the Russian intellectual tradition, and the "woman question"—the problem of how to improve women's situation—became a standard topic in discussions of Russian reform. Not surprisingly, the reformers' definitions of women's emancipation varied, from cautious proposals merely to educate them better to vigorous demands for their participation in society as men's equals.

It was primarily men—intellectuals and artists—who shaped the increasingly fashionable conception of woman as suffering servant, but it was primarily women who led the efforts to improve women's situation. Most of the feminists of the 1860s and 1870s came from elite backgrounds. Maria Trubnikova, Anna Filosofova, and Nadezda Stasova, the three most prominent members of the first generation of Russian feminists, were members of the cultural elite of St. Petersburg. Later, as educational opportunities for women expanded, the ranks of feminists were increasingly enlarged by women from the lesser nobility, and continued to draw a few from the burgeoning middle class and a very few peasants.

Russian feminism had much in common with that elsewhere in Europe and North America. Feminists everywhere at this time tended to be privileged, for only such people had the resources and leisure to devote to political organizing. Russia's feminists, like their counterparts in the West, addressed themselves particularly to the situation of poor women, while also concerning themselves with many larger questions connected with the reformation of society in general. They often worked hard in charitable projects such as relief of the poor and the rehabilitation of prostitutes, as well as in efforts to expand educational and professional opportunities for better-off women like themselves.

Charity could do little to remedy the overwhelming poverty of Russia's cities and villages, however. It was the recognition of this bitter reality that impelled many feminists in the 1870s to concentrate on the struggle for higher education for women. Here they achieved limited but genuine improvements. After years of petitioning the government (which controlled education as it controlled so much else), the feminists had managed by 1880 to establish "higher women's courses" in St. Petersburg, Moscow, Kazan, and Kiev. Faculty from the universities volunteered their time to teach the young women who hungered for higher education, and organizers raised money from the wealthy to rent lecture halls and provide stipends for needy students. The sponsors struggled under enormous difficulties, for not only was financial support hard to come by, but the government remained hostile, closing down the courses for most of the 1880s, and only reluctantly permitting them to reopen thereafter. Despite such obstacles, thousands of young women were graduated by 1900 and were working as teachers and doctors in schools and hospitals that served the urban poor as well as the peasants.

Not surprisingly, many of these graduates also became reform feminists or revolutionaries.

Revolution, the most drastic solution to society's problems, appealed to a few, very daring Russian women. Would-be revolutionaries, like the feminists, were primarily well-educated women, though they were often less wellborn, less likely to hail from the most privileged families, than the feminists. Most female revolutionaries came from the lower nobility in the 1860s and 1870s, and, by the 1890s, from the middle ranks of urban society as well. All of them were socialists who rejected feminism as too unconcerned with the problems of the poor and too slow to recognize the inadequacy of piecemeal reform. Root-and-branch reformers, convinced that destruction was indispensable to renewal, they believed that only the establishment of an egalitarian society based on common ownership of property would make possible the equality of all women and men. This socialist critique of feminism, like the larger socialist vision connected with it, was widespread in Europe; it had particular appeal in Russia because the backwardness and intractability of the autocratic government made reform seem like mere tinkering with a worthless vessel.

Intent on stirring the peasants to rebellion, hundreds of young women joined the thousands of young men engaged in illegal revolutionary activities from the late 1860s through the 1890s. They wrote and circulated pamphlets criticizing the government, gathered together groups of students and factory workers to study socialist ideas, and participated in strikes and demonstrations. A few female revolutionaries also became terrorists. All these projects did little to provoke popular uprisings, but they did create a tradition of female involvement in the revolutionary movement and they nourished the intelligentsia's belief in woman's capacity for heroic self-sacrifice. The most notorious revolutionary women of that age were the assassins—Sofia Perovskaia, hanged in 1881 for her participation in the assassination of Alexander II, and Vera Zasulich, tried and acquitted in 1878 for the attempted assassination of a tsarist governor. Vera Figner and Ekaterina Breshko-Breshkovskaia also became famous, mainly because they survived decades in solitary confinement in tsarist prisons. Figner was sent there for her part in several assassinations, Breshko-Breshkovskaia for attempting to stir up peasant revolts. Each endured a brutally harsh prison regimen for twenty-two years, remained unrepentant, and on release resumed her revolutionary activity. Socially conscious Russians adorned their walls with engravings of the solemn faces of these earnest young women, so intent on self-sacrifice for radical political and social change.

Women of the Middle Classes

Revolutionary women, although widely admired by the liberal intelligentsia, were, of course, only a tiny minority among women in Russia in the second half of the nineteenth century. Most noblewomen stayed away from reform efforts and confined their activities to their families. So too did women of the middle levels of society. This group, very small so long as Russia remained a rural country little involved in commerce, began to grow in the nineteenth century when manufacturing, trade, and the professions expanded. The middling classes of Russia's cities were made up from old merchant families, peasants newly transformed into capitalists, the children of priests, Jews, and a smattering of people from other non-Slavic ethnic groups. They ranged in occupation from traders and manufacturers to shopkeepers, physicians, and teachers. They were in fact too heterogenous to be called a class, but their social significance was growing. From their ranks came many of those who joined, and then rose to lead, the reform movements that flourished after 1900.

The women of this sector of society differed as substantially from one another as did the men, but many of them shared a need to find "respectable" white-collar work. In the 1880s and 1890s it became customary for the young women of Russia's urban middle class to get a secondary education and then work until marriage as clerks, shop attendants, teachers, feldshers (physicians' assistants), midwives, and dentists. There were far fewer such middle-class working women in Russia than in contemporary Britain and the United States, thanks to the much slower pace in Russia of industrialization and urbanization. But this group was to play a role in the revolutionary era disproportionate to its numbers.

Peasant Women

Change came far more slowly to the ramshackle villages scattered across the great plains and forests of Russia's empire. There peasant women continued to observe the centuries-old patterns of the agricultural year, the patterns of planting and gathering, of lambing and calving. They still baked dark rye bread, still drew water from wells in their barnyards, still stood with other women in the dim light of midnight masses, and hunted with them for mushrooms when spring came. They still birthed one another's babies and crooned laments for the dead. Their lives were bounded by the horizon, by the expanses of fields, meadows, and woods that they had played in and harvested since childhood. In the past what little they had known of the world beyond came to them when peddlers and pilgrims, tax collectors and military recruiters, appeared at their gates.

But in the late nineteenth century even peasant women began to be affected by the changes emanating from cities such as Moscow and St. Petersburg, Warsaw and Kiev. Now they could buy factory-made goods—tools, pots, nails, cloth, even ribbons. Many peasants, mostly male, learned to read in village schools. People travelled back and forth between the countryside and the cities, and every summer young men on vacation from their factory jobs swaggered through the village streets sporting bright new city-bought shirts and bragging that they were not going to let their mothers choose their wives for them.

Peasant women knew vaguely about the new world emerging in the cities, but most of them remained warily at a distance from it. A small number of women moved away from the villages in the late nineteenth century, migrating to the urban areas to work as servants, or, by the 1880s, as factory workers. But these were very much in the minority. The elders in the villages, women as well as men, hewed to the age-old custom of keeping younger women at home while the young men went away. This adaptation of traditional practices to a new situation made economic sense. The government had burdened the peasants with heavy debts, payment for the land ceded to them during Emancipation, debts for which entire families were responsible. A family could not legally move from the village until those debts were paid, and since most peasants were far too poor to raise the necessary money, they had to stay on in the countryside and till the land. So the young men travelled off to work in the factories, sending home part of their wages and returning several times a year to visit and to help with the harvest; their wives meanwhile worked with the family. As a result of male migration the cities began to swell with men, while the villages of central Russia became disproportionately female.

This adaptation to industrialization held significant consequences for women. Men of the European nationalities (the Slavs, Baltic peoples, and Jews) went away to learn skilled work that paid better wages than subsistence farming; women remained in the villages to assume an increasing share of the farmwork. Such changes resulted in predictable adjustments to social ideology. Although neither peasant men nor peasant women had ever had anything to do before with industrial machinery, both soon came to believe that men were better suited to work with machines and that women should stick to manual labor. Peasant males justified taking the best jobs in industry by saying that women were too backward to learn how to operate lathes or blast furnaces. It was in no small measure due to these firm new convictions that even when substantial numbers of women did enter the factories in the early twentieth century, they could not move beyond unskilled jobs that paid less than subsistence wages. Meanwhile, back on the farm, as mechanization came to the countryside, men climbed aboard the reapers and left women stooped over pulling up sugar beets. Male control over the opportunities offered by industrialization may have developed in part because of the strength required to run larger machinery (the peasants had always allocated the heaviest work to men). It was affected by the economic exigencies of the late nineteenth century. But it was also a consequence of the fact that the peasants were attempting as best they knew how to control the effects of modernization on village society by preserving the established patriarchal order, and particularly its governance of women.

CONCLUSIONS

The legacy of the nineteenth century for women in the Russian Empire was complex. The women of all the many ethnic groups inherited from traditional society a position and roles that were circumscribed by patriarchy, but they also enjoyed limited influence, respect, a sphere of authority, and a cluster of beliefs and habits that validated their work and their world. When upper-class women of the European population began to depart from tradition with the spread of modernizing ideas and practices in the eighteenth and nineteenth centuries, most of them did so in ways that did not frontally challenge fundamental patriarchal institutions. Similarly, in the countryside in the late nineteenth century the peasants carefully limited the effects of modernization on women. At the same time, however, a group of upper-class primarily Russian women, sometimes in combination with men, began to mount a more thoroughgoing challenge to the status quo. They put the woman question on the reform agenda, and thereafter women joined men in reform and revolutionary movements. By the end of the nineteenth century, therefore, while peasant women throughout the Empire were still living much as their ancient forbearers had done, women in the major cities were beginning to find themselves torn between the demands of tradition and the new cries for reform that were coming increasingly from the ranks of women themselves, from revolutionaries, social reformers, and from factory workers. This conflict was embedded in the larger struggle to reform all of Russia, a struggle that finally led to revolution in 1917.

2 / THE REVOLUTIONARY ERA

1890–1921

By the end of the nineteenth century, economic and political pressures were building up in the Russian Empire because of the government's inability to manage modernization. Instead of relieving the miserable poverty of the countryside, industrialization had spawned a poverty-stricken working class living in the cities but retaining strong ties to the villages. The workers increasingly demanded improvements in living and working conditions for which employers usually refused to pay. The government backed the employers. Intellectuals, frustrated by their political powerlessness, circulated among the workers, some trying to ameliorate the miseries with charitable projects, others exhorting people to revolt. Alarmed by the growing agitation for reform, the tsarist government responded with repression, and succeeded in convincing even moderates that nothing short of major political change would improve the situation.

This ferment, in which millions of women participated, climaxed in a revolution in 1917 that destroyed both the monarchy and the nobility. The revolution in turn had momentous consequences for women. Most important, it brought to power the Bolshevik wing of the Russian Social-Democratic Labor Party.[1] The Party, which had committed itself to reforms for women before the revolution, began to pursue a broad program for women's emancipation from traditional social strictures soon after seizing power. Meanwhile the years of domestic turmoil and war were destroying the Russian economy and making most women's lives much more difficult. Women's reactions to the revolu-

---

1 The Bolsheviks changed the name of their organization to the Russian Communist Party in 1918. With the establishment of the Soviet Union in the early 1920s, the official party title became the Communist Party of the Soviet Union.

tion naturally varied according to their positions in society, their individual circumstances, and the odds they perceived of benefiting or losing from this great sea-change. But in view of what many women had endured earlier, it is understandable that millions attached themselves fervently to what the new seemed to promise.

WOMEN AND THE PRESSURE FOR REFORM

Working-class Women

The unrest that led to revolution was centered in Russia's cities, not in the countryside, and in the European west of the Empire rather than in Siberia, the Caucasus, or Central Asia. Consequently, peasant women of all the many nationalities contributed little to the overthrow of the Romanov dynasty. Far more significant was the small but growing female working class that first appeared in central Russia in the 1880s, as women began moving into the towns seeking jobs. Overwhelmingly they were European in ethnicity, for industrialization came first to the European part of the Empire. The migrants might be Jewish, Polish, or Latvian teenagers from rural families too poor to keep their daughters with them in the villages. They might be Russian or Ukrainian widows unable to support themselves any longer in agriculture. Most of these women, when they reached cities such as Riga or Odessa, went to work as servants in the households of the nobility. Living under the close supervision of their employers, maids and cooks could not easily get caught up in protest activities. Female factory workers were less sheltered. As early as the 1880s women were filling up the unskilled jobs in the textile mills of Moscow and Ivanovo-Voznesensk. By the first decade of the twentieth century, women were also working in paper and tobacco manufacturing, in chemical- and mineral-processing, and in service enterprises such as restaurants, bakeries, and laundries in large cities and small towns. Women by 1914 made up 32 percent of Russia's industrial labor force, one of the highest percentages in Europe. The numbers of women in the population of the city of Moscow rose a staggering 57 percent in the fifteen years between 1897 and 1912.

Sadly, this move to the city did little to improve women's lives. Throughout Europe, domestic servants earned very low wages for long hours of hard work. Humane people provided their employees with decent living quarters, food, and medical care and gave them regular time off. Working for such people was an improvement over the destitution in the villages that forced most women to migrate to the cities. If the women were less fortunate, however, they ended up with inhumane people who worked them from dawn to midnight, allowed them to eat only table scraps, made them sleep in corners, refused them any leisure time, and sexually harassed them. Even the most liberal employers denied servants the right to keep their jobs after they married and routinely fired any who became pregnant out of wedlock.

Conditions for women in the factories were as bad, if not worse. Female factory workers were paid less than men and denied opportunities to learn how to perform the better-paying jobs. The result, the daily pain and horror of living on the edge of destitution, is recorded in bleak statistics. Factory inspectors in the early twentieth century calculated that the wages of a woman worker in St. Petersburg were below subsistence levels. This meant that a woman, with what she earned at the factory, could not afford housing and sufficient food to maintain her health. Nor was the work for which she was so miserably paid easy. Typical were twelve- to fourteen-hour days at hard manual labor in dirty, poorly ventilated buildings, crowded with noisy, dangerous machinery. Textile workers coped with high heat and humidity, chemical workers with toxic substances. Although there were exemplary industrialists such as the Armands of Moscow, who built decent housing and operated schools for their workers, most of Russia's early capitalists refused even to grant sick leave. With a huge labor pool to draw on and under little government pressure to do otherwise, they treated their workers far less considerately than they did their machinery. For many women the consequences were poverty and ruined health.

Factory workers and domestic servants also contended with sexual abuse. Inadequate wages, highly seasonal work, and frequent layoffs forced some women into prostitution in order to survive. Even those not so desperate confronted a great deal of sexual abuse in the cities, where they did not have the defenses that traditional society provided in the form of retaliation by irate male relatives against rapists and attackers. Women in the factories were routinely patted, fondled, and even strip-searched by their foremen and other bosses; in the working-class slums where they lived, they had to contend with men who considered a woman living on her own fair game. Female servants were at risk of sexual harassment by their employers. It is not difficult to understand, therefore, why working-class women sought to get married and leave their jobs. As their mothers and grand-mothers had done in the villages, they advised one another to seek out sober, good-tempered husbands with steady employment.

But even after marriage, life remained a struggle. Working-class men were not well paid, and they too were subject to fre-quent layoffs as well as working conditions that left many disabled, chronically ill, unhappy, frustrated, and abusive. The slums were miserable places to live, rife with alcoholism, fam-ily violence, and abandonment. Thus most working-class women found that marriage was not so much an escape as an alternative pattern of difficulties. Many continued to work in the factories until the birth of their first, second, or third child, arranging for neighbors to tend their infants or even leaving them alone for extended periods. Only the most impoverished women re-mained at factory work once they had borne several babies, though poverty forced continuation of such work more often in Russia than elsewhere in the industrialized world. Working-class mothers, if their husbands' wages were insufficient to keep the family going, would take in laundry, do finishing sewing for garment factories, or tend to others' children. Such work, though miserably paid, could be performed while caring for their own babies, and it was often less gruelling physically than factory work. When their children were old enough, they put them to work as well. Girls did piece work (sewing collars on shirts, for example) or babysat, until they were old enough to find jobs themselves in the factories.

The childhoods of Klavdia Nikolaeva and Anna Artiukhina were typical. Both were born into working-class families, Niko-laeva in St. Petersburg, Artiukhina in a smaller city, Vyshnyi Volochek, near Moscow. When the two were very young, in the mid-1890s, their fathers left home, and their mothers, textile workers, had to struggle to feed the children on their meager wages. Nikolaeva was a determined, intelligent child who taught herself to read and then managed to attend an elementary school in the Petersburg slums, where she learned a little geography and mathematics. In her early teens she went to work at a printing press. Artiukhina also began working at a young age, sewing shirts at home. Her mother could not afford to let Anna go to school, and the family's situation got still worse when she was fired for being involved in union activities. They all moved to St. Petersburg, where Anna's uncle lived. By now Anna was fifteen, and she and her mother both found jobs in the mills.

Born into a world where poverty was inescapable, thwarted by a government unable and generally unwilling to reform the economic system, some working-class women, the great majority of them factory workers, took their anger to the streets of Riga, Warsaw, Ivanovo-Voznesensk, Odessa, and other cities between 1890 and 1917. Women workers organized strikes; textile and tobacco workers were particularly known for large walkouts involving hundreds of people. Thousands marched in demonstrations against the government in 1905 in St. Petersburg and Moscow and signed petitions demanding the vote. But most women were reluctant to take the next step in protest—joining a trade union or a political party. Artiukhina and Nikolaeva both were union members, but they were unusual women. Women made up less than 10 percent of all unionists when the tsarist government permitted unions to operate legally after 1905. Only a handful served on union governing boards, and even the leadership of the textile workers was predominantly male. (Again there is a correspondence here between Russia's experience and that elsewhere, where men, despite women's predominance in this or that specialized workforce, almost universally headed union organizations.) Working-class women also stayed away from moderate and radical political organizations. Fewer than half the female Social Democrats in the prerevolutionary years were working-class in origin.

This pattern of many women taking part in short-lived uprisings such as strikes or demonstrations but few women participating in formal organizations prevailed across Europe in the nineteenth and early twentieth centuries. In general, women were less politically active than men, less willing to march in demonstrations, less willing to become involved in trade unions or political parties. Indeed, wives sometimes implored their husbands not to have any contact with such organizations. Political activists, moderates and revolutionaries alike, attributed this to women's conservatism, which, they believed, resulted from women's being less educated and more religious than men.

But in blaming women, radicals and reformers alike ignored the fact that their own organizations actually discouraged women from joining, because of the widespread opinion among unionists and politicians that women did not belong in unions, parties, or even in the factories, for that matter. In part this resistance to women entering the public world of work and politics developed because women competed with men for jobs; unfairly, some believed. Employers, eager to lower the cost of doing business, paid women less than men, considered them more manageable than men, and thus whenever possible hired them to replace men. Many trade unionists and middle-class radicals, therefore, believed that women complicated the already difficult task of organizing factory workers.

Trade unionists and middle-class radicals also argued that women would be better off if they never did hard labor in dirty, dangerous factories. Rather, women should aspire to live as middle-class women did, tending lovely homes, rearing healthy children, and sheltering their hard-working menfolk. This idealization of women as homemakers came originally from the very propertied middle class against whom radicals and trade unionists struggled, but it had great appeal to all the people of the cities in the nineteenth century.

Perceiving women's entry into politics or the paid labor force as disruptive, wishing them rather to remain in the more traditional position of housekeeper and dependent of men, very few politicians of nineteenth-century Europe, whether reactionary, conservative, liberal or radical, welcomed women into their chambers and board meetings. The reformers and the radicals justified their attitudes by declaring that women were unhappily too passive and too ignorant to be of much help. Of course working-class women were able to figure all this out. Indeed it was abundantly clear that men did not want them joining unions or political parties. Many women persuaded themselves to accept the male evaluation; they adopted the view that politics was a male sphere. Other women, genuinely as conservative as the reformers charged, clung to traditional values. Still others simply feared reformist politics because of the potentially high cost to their income, security, and family life. Hence the easiest course for all but the most radical working-class women was to join from time to time in angry outbursts—riots, strikes, demonstrations—but to steer clear of the men's organizations. Unwritten understandings thus grew up between working women and radical organizers, and the latter, even females among them, concentrated their efforts almost exclusively on organizing men. As Cecelia Bobrovskaia, a Russian Social Democrat, wrote, "It never occurred to us to carry on work among them [women]; the job seemed such a thankless one. Besides, there was so much other work which we could barely cope with that agitation among the women was left for more favorable times."[2] Those times eventually came, but misperceptions between revolutionaries and the masses of working-class women persisted long into the Soviet era.

Women of the Intelligentsia

Less troubled was the relationship between women and men within the intelligentsia, the educated elite of professionals, artists and writers among whom reformist and revolutionary ideas flourished. The intelligentsia had long been critical of Russian patriarchy and had long welcomed women into its ranks. In the early twentieth century, women of the intelligentsia were politically active as reformers and revolutionaries.

The feminist activities of the late nineteenth century—charity among working-class women, support for higher education for more privileged ones—continued until 1905. In the 1890s, increasing numbers of women with professional aspirations and strong feminist sentiments found employment all across the vast country as teachers and medical workers. They participated in feminist organizations in St. Petersburg and Moscow and supported the efforts of their reform-minded male comrades in the

---

2 Cecelia Bobrovskaia, *Twenty Years in Underground Russia* (New York, 1934), 109.

legal and medical professions to pressure the government into addressing problems connected with public health and working conditions. The largest and most effective feminist organization was the Russian Mutual Philanthropic Society, organized in 1895 and led by a physician, Anna Shabanova. The Society, headquartered in St. Petersburg, ran day-care centers and restaurants catering to impoverished middle-class women.

The year 1905 was a time of explosive protests, ignited by humiliating losses in the Russo-Japanese War of 1904-1905 and by ongoing economic and political problems. During this upheaval a new generation of feminist leaders emerged from the ranks of professional women. The revolutionary spirit of 1905 made it possible for them to be more militant than their predecessors, and they were inspired as well by the success of determined feminists in Great Britain, the United States, and nearby Finland. They established the All-Russian Union for Women's Equality, which began to press for the vote for women, as well as for attention to the problems of the poor. The feminists of the Union held marches, demonstrations, and meetings in the major cities, and lobbied male members of the newly established political parties. They also began reaching out to lower-class women by sending organizers among them to preach women's rights and to gather petitions for women's suffrage. In December 1905 another feminist organization, the Women's Progressive Party, was founded by physician Maria Pokrovskaia. This group was less militant on suffrage than the Union, but more vocal in calling for reforms for working-class women.

Despite their best efforts, however, neither the Union for Women's Equality nor the Women's Progressive Party was able to establish a strong political base. Their campaigns to recruit working-class women failed because of the great gulf that divided the educated and privileged from the poor in Russia; neither side really trusted or understood the other. Even the men of their own classes were uncertain allies, for leaders of both moderate and radical political parties hesitated to endorse women's suffrage, arguing that it would be unwise to give the vote to conservative, ignorant lower-class women. Support for the feminists, lukewarm at best, cooled still further as the government regained its political strength after 1905 and began to curtail the political liberties it had been forced to grant to men during the revolutionary upsurge.

The Union for Women's Equality (and its successor, named in 1907 the League for Equal Rights), the Women's Progressive Party, and the Mutual Philanthropic Society continued to push for reforms after 1905, calling conferences to publicize issues such as prostitution control, education for women, and legal rights. The high point of their activities came in 1908 when a general meeting brought a thousand delegates to St. Petersburg. The conference revealed all the strengths and weaknesses of the intelligentsia's advocacy of the woman question. Delegates conducted a searching analysis of the origins of women's situation, dissecting Russian patriarchal traditions as well as the negative consequences of industrialization. But they could reach no agreement on solutions to the problems they identified, because they themselves were split into factions of revolutionaries and feminists that spent much of the conference insulting one another. Furthermore, the government had only granted permission for the conference on the condition that a whole series of politically sensitive issues, such as land reform, not be discussed. Policemen were stationed in the hall to monitor all the debates, and they cleared their throats or shifted ominously in their chairs when forbidden subjects were mentioned. Even if the conference delegates had managed to pass resolutions, moreover, they had no power to affect government policy.

In subsequent years, the feminists' lobbying did bring about a few improvements: in 1912 the government issued a decree establishing equal inheritance rights for women in real and moveable property (excepting land); and in 1914 it granted women the right to hold passports in their own names. The fact that relatively insignificant changes required decades of exhausting petitioning and agitation was eloquent testimony to the difficulty of achieving reform for women in tsarist Russia.

This lesson was not lost on Russia's revolutionaries, of course. Indeed, the inability of reform-minded feminists to build a stronger movement confirmed for more radical women their conviction that feminism was an inadequate response to the injustices of Russian society. Those women who became revolutionaries before 1917 had a number of illegal organizations to choose from, the largest of which were the Social-Democratic Party (SDs) and the Socialist Revolutionary Party (SRs). The SDs were Marxists who concentrated their hopes and organizing efforts on the industrial workers. The SRs, also strongly influenced by Marxism but loyal to nineteenth-century Russian socialism, reached out to the peasantry as well as to urban workers. Both groups had female members, though it is impossible to determine how many since these underground organizations kept few records. Fragmentary evidence suggests that 10 to 15 percent of both were women.

There were strong similarities between these women and the two previous generations of female revolutionaries, the hundreds who had struggled alongside Perovskaia, Zasulich, Figner, and Breshko-Breshkovskaia. Like them, most early twentieth-century female revolutionaries came from the nobility or middle class, though a few were workers. More now hailed from Jewish, Polish, Latvian, and other non-Russian ethnic groups. Like the feminists, many of these more radical women had trained to be teachers or medical workers, and many had worked for a time in those "caring" professions before becoming convinced that only revolution could cure Russia's ills.

Until 1917, the SRs and the SDs spent most of their time spreading their gospel among factory workers by distributing pamphlets and leaflets and by organizing "circles" of workers to study revolutionary ideology. During periods of social unrest they tried to assume leadership over striking workers or students, but generally until 1917 they were unsuccessful. The tsarist police were so adept at finding and arresting revolutionaries that neither the SRs nor the SDs could maintain anything more than the most ephemeral and therefore ineffective organizations.

Women served in the Russian revolutionary underground mostly as spear-carriers and foot soldiers. Male revolutionaries, in keeping with the idealistic philosophies of equality and freedom which all revolutionaries devoutly shared, attempted to treat their female counterparts as comrades and made few distinctions between men's and women's revolutionary work. Female Social Democrats assembled bombs in 1905, and female Socialist Revolutionaries assassinated tsarist officials. Leadership, however, was another matter. Men ran the underground parties, particularly at the national level. Only one woman, the SR Maria

Spiridonova, rose to a position of genuine leadership in a revolutionary organization, and she may have owed her prominence to the fact that she was adored as a revolutionary martyr, a role women had played since Perovskaia's time. Spiridonova murdered a particularly loathsome general, survived a ferocious beating while under arrest, and then endured years in prison. There were no female SDs of comparable note, perhaps because the SDs condemned terrorism as ineffectual. Some female SDs led local party committees, and a few were important members of the circles of expatriate radicals living abroad to stay out of the clutches of the police. The best known of this latter group was Nadezhda Krupskaia, the wife of V. I. Lenin, leader of the Bolshevik wing of the Social-Democratic Party; her job was to manage communications between the Party leaders in Western Europe and underground workers in Russia. Yet despite the fact that women did not figure prominently among SR or SD leaders, the world of the revolutionaries was, by comparison with the larger Russian society, unusual as a place where women routinely experienced respect, creativity, even freedom.

Until 1917 the revolutionaries achieved no more in the way of tangible reforms for women than the feminists. Pressures for reform did threaten the regime in 1905, but the tsar, bending to popular cries, managed to ride out the storm. In the years that followed, his ministers made every effort to reassert his autocratic prerogatives. For a time they succeeded, but then in 1914 the government stumbled, bluffed, and trapped itself into World War I. At first patriotism muted the people's discontentment, but in a few months devastating losses at the front and mounting hardships at home touched off more unrest. This time the government could find no way out of its predicament, and the more it thrashed around, the more the anger against it grew.

WOMEN IN THE REVOLUTION—THE SPARK

The Russian Revolution began in February 1917 with scattered strikes and demonstrations in Petrograd.[3] By this time, three

---

3 The name of Russia's capital city was changed from St. Petersburg to Petrograd in 1914. In 1918 the capital was moved to Moscow. In 1924 Petrograd was renamed Leningrad, but it became St. Petersburg again in 1991.

years of bloody war had left more than 7 million military casualties. Shortages of food and consumer goods had become very
serious, owing to the military preoccupation of the country's
industrial and communications systems. Inflation had then
driven up the prices of what little food was available.

By January of 1917, bakeries in Petrograd were desperately
short of bread, the mainstay of poor people's diets. Shopping
was women's work; so it was women who stood in long lines
waiting for bread in the dark early hours of frozen January
mornings. Sometimes when they found that prices had risen
again, or when the meager supplies sold out quickly, they rioted,
shouting, shoving, and throwing stones through the shop windows. A prescient officer in the Okhrana, the police department
in charge of political offenses, reported to the Minister of In-
terior in January 1917: "The mothers of families, who are exhausted by the endless standing in line at the stores, who are
worn out by the suffering of seeing their children half-starved
and sick, may now be much closer to revolution than Mr.
Miliukov, Rodzianko and Company [leaders of the Duma,
Russia's parliament], and of course, they are much more dangerous, since they represent a store of combustible material. One
spark would be enough for a conflagration to blaze up."[4]

The war had been no kinder to the villages than to the cities. True, in the countryside there was more food than in town.
Urban shortages resulted primarily from two causes, the peasants'
refusal to sell grain at prices held artificially low by the government, and breakdowns in the transportation system. But the war
brought both spiritual and economic hardship to the villages,
for the military drafted more than 10 million peasant men. Most
of Russia's millions of dead and wounded were peasants. Furthermore, the departure of the men meant what it always had
for women, namely that they had to do the work of those who
left in addition to their own. Since this male migration was much
larger than any in the past, it increased women's burdens significantly. For many, the loss of their menfolk also meant a significant drop in income, a drop not made up by the paltry
military allotments paid to soldiers' wives. It was ironic and tragic

---

4 Quoted in Z. Igumnova, *Zhenshchiny Moskvy v gody grazhdanskoi voiny* (Moscow, 1958), 11.

that the *soldatki*, the wives of those serving in the army, were thus doubly impoverished by the war.

Some women responded to the crisis by seeking work in the cities, where the same conscription that had drained manpower from the villages was opening up jobs in industry. Between 1914 and 1917 the number of women rose from 26 to 43 percent of the industrial labor force, with the numbers increasing even more substantially in sectors once predominantly male, such as metalworking. Women were 3 percent of metalworkers in 1913; by 1916 they made up 18 percent of that industry's workers. For a few women these new opportunities meant an improvement in their standard of living, at least initially, but as inflation and shortages developed in the cities, even well-paid workers began to suffer.

Women of the middle class and nobility were protected longer than were the poor from the war's economic consequences, because they had savings accounts and other economic resources to draw on. Educated women who had to support themselves could move into white-collar jobs once held by men. But wealth did not protect noble and middle-class women from the loss of their male relatives, nor inure them to the government's incompetence. Disaffection spread among them as well. It was, however, just as the Okhrana official had predicted, working-class women who set off the "conflagration" that became the Russian Revolution.

February 23 (March 8 by the Western calendar) was International Woman's Day, a day designated by the Second Socialist International in 1910 as a time for socialists to demonstrate for women's suffrage. In Russia, committees of female Social Democrats had held large gatherings on Woman's Day in 1913 and 1914. Their chief organizer was Konkordia Samoilova, an editor of the Bolshevik newspaper *Pravda*, a gentle and persuasive woman who had grown up the daughter of a priestly family in Siberia and had become a revolutionary while attending the university courses for women in St. Petersburg in the late 1890s. Arrested in 1914, she was exiled far from the capital until after the revolution began in 1917. With Samoilova gone, no one bothered to organize meetings for International Woman's Day, though Party workers in Petrograd did publish leaflets addressed to women on February 23 in 1915 and 1916. In 1917 they did

the same: leaflets blaming women's hardships on the government appeared in workers' neighborhoods in mid-February.
There were also a few small meetings for women workers held
a few days before February 23. But the revolutionaries had no
particular plans for Woman's Day itself.

They were as surprised as anyone, therefore, when working-
class women began pouring out of the factories in the early
morning of February 23, chanting "Bread!" and "End the war!"
It has never been clear who ignited this outburst, but once it
began, crowds of angry women swarmed through the narrow
streets in several of Petrograd's industrial areas, stopping at
factory windows to call for the workers inside to join them. By
midday, groups of women and teenagers had gathered at the
bridges over the Neva River and were trying to charge through
police lines to take their demonstration to the Nevskii Prospekt,
the great boulevard that ran through the center of the city. When
they could not fight their way across the bridges, they clambered
down the river bank and slipped across the ice. Elsewhere,
women rioted outside bakeries and pelted factory windows with
rocks. Toward sunset the unusually warm weather changed,
temperatures fell rapidly, and the crowds dispersed. But perhaps
as many as 120,000 people had heard the women's calls and
walked off their jobs that day. The demonstrations grew still
larger on subsequent days; the troops called out to quell them
mutinied; and reinforcements sent from the front mutinied as
well. On March 2, the tsar bowed to the demands of the crowds
and the request of his own generals, and abdicated.

WOMEN IN THE REVOLUTION—MARCH TO OCTOBER

The revolution quickly spread from Petrograd to other cities,
to Moscow, Saratov, Warsaw, Kiev, and into Siberia to Tomsk and
eastward. Demonstrators attacked government offices and drove
officials out of town. Soon members of the Duma had set up a
provisional government, while representatives of trade unions
and the socialist parties organized elected assemblies called
soviets to represent the lower classes. With central authority gone,
the economy deteriorated still further. But more important, the
entire remaining structure of power throughout the Russian

Empire began to collapse. By late spring, soldiers, workers, and peasants by the millions were defying officers, factory owners, and landlords. Military desertions rose, strikes became increasingly common, and in the countryside, peasants began pressuring the nobles to give up their land. By midsummer, independence movements were sweeping through Finland, the Baltic provinces, Poland, Ukraine, and the Caucasus.

Women were involved in every aspect of the upheaval of 1917. To uncover what they did, and why, it is useful first to consider their attitudes toward the revolution, and then to analyze their participation in strikes, demonstrations, riots, and land confiscations, as well as in formal organizations, particularly trade unions and political parties. Such an analysis requires careful differentiation of women's attitudes and behavior according to social class and ethnicity, for these affiliations affected their responses to 1917 as strongly as did their gender.

Women's Attitudes Toward the Revolution

At first many noblewomen welcomed the fall of the monarchy. However, as the revolution spread from attacks on the tsarist government to more general assaults on the privileges of the upper classes (something which began to occur in the late spring and early summer of 1917), most upper-class women became convinced that the process was going desperately wrong. Political opinion within the nobility shaded off between conservatism on the one hand and liberal reformism on the other, but even the most reform-minded nobles understandably became less enthusiastic for change as the year advanced and peasants began seizing their property. By the fall of 1917, noblewomen by the hundreds of thousands had abandoned their estates and were fleeing abroad or to the borderlands where anticommunist armies were forming. Only the noblewomen of those areas that broke free of the Russian Empire—the Baltic states, Finland, and Poland—managed to survive the revolution with their titles and social positions intact. Consequently, most noblewomen condemned the revolution as a monumental disaster, which, for them, it most certainly was.

The middling orders of urban society were more divided in their loyalties and opinions. It was from this sector that most of the female revolutionaries came; but then so did the feminists. Many middle-class women were liberal in their political thinking; they favored some form of democratic, constitutional government. By the fall of 1917, they became alarmed by the growing power of the radical socialists, particularly the Bolshevik wing of the Social Democratic Party, and supported instead efforts by the Prime Minister of the Provisional Government, Alexander Kerensky, to build a coalition of centrist political groups.

Feminist organizations, particularly the League for Equal Rights, were revitalized by the revolution, and in a short time made substantial gains from it. Many Russian feminists, like their counterparts in other countries, had worked nobly as volunteers in the war effort, and, also like feminists in Britain or the United States, they expected to be rewarded for their service with the vote. After the February Revolution, Russia's liberal and socialist parties did indeed write women's suffrage into their platforms. When the Provisional Government failed to mention votes for women in its first declaration of political liberties, therefore, League members began bombarding its ministers with petitions. They also quickly set up affiliated organizations in most of Russia's major cities, as they had done in 1905, and initiated a broad campaign to build support among working-class women. By midsummer the Provisional Government had responded by establishing universal suffrage, writing new laws permitting women to practice law and serve as jurors, and declaring a policy of equal opportunity for women in the civil service. These reforms only strengthened the commitment of many middle-class women to the liberal political agenda developed before World War I.

As the revolutionaries had always charged, however, liberalism offered little to lighten the burdens borne by working-class women. Instead, the poor stood to benefit from the dismantling of the powers and property of the privileged. Thus many of them welcomed the attack on the nobility. It is certain that some, particularly the young, also felt what can only be called a wild thrill, a rush of personal liberation that came with the sense that all established institutions, including those that kept women in thrall, were crashing down. Alexandra Rodionova, a twenty-two-year-old tram conductor in 1917, described her euphoria this way: "I had the feeling that I had been picked up by a mighty, powerful wave and lifted ever higher and higher, to a point where I could see everything all around me."[5] People in such a mood felt called upon to join unions and revolutionary political parties in order to give their energies to the great cause.

Most working-class women did not go so far, however. Some were frightened by the revolution, just as they had been frightened in the past by any disruption that threatened their survival. But even those working women who applauded the rush of political change had to concentrate their energies on their jobs and on providing for their families. Since these tasks became increasingly difficult in 1917 as the economy continued to decline, more and more of women's time was absorbed in them, leaving less than before for political involvement. Furthermore, inasmuch as it was difficult even for literate people to sort out all the political parties and keep track of their ideological shifts as the year progressed, many illiterate ones—and this included the majority of working women—simply did not try. Most working women made their way through 1917 buffeted by vague hopes, real fears, overwork, hardship, and extreme confusion. They took comfort in small pleasures and triumphs, and, if they were lucky, they were spared the searing personal pain of losing loved ones.

The condition of peasant women is in some ways less clear than this, but it appears that many of them, like peasant men, welcomed the overthrow of the tsar. They heartily supported the confiscation of the nobles' land that occurred in the summer and fall, but few seem to have entertained any notions about changing the rules that regulated village life.

It is even less clear how the women of Central Asia and the Caucasus felt about the revolution. In both regions new leaders sprang up to struggle for power, some leading independence movements, others seeking affiliation with Russian political organizations. The turmoil did not end until the early 1920s, when the Soviet government established its control over both areas, but none of this upheaval had much impact on the in-

---

5 A. Rodionova, "Vash korrespondent," *Vsegda s vami; sbornik posviashchennyi 50-letiiu zhurnala "Rabotnitsa"* (Moscow, 1964), 101.

ALEXANDRA KOLLONTAI

Alexandra Kollontai was one of the most important socialist feminists of her generation, the author of many books and articles that promoted the Marxist analysis of women's emancipation. She contributed to that analysis a heartfelt appreciation of the ways in which women and men were conditioned psychologically to accept their positions in society. Only when women had learned not to subordinate themselves in intimate relationships with men would they achieve true independence and equality, Kollontai argued. Her advocacy of women's psychological liberation and her exploration of the means to that end in articles, monographs, short stories, and novels made her well known throughout Europe in the 1920s, and led to a revival of interest in her with the revival of feminism in the 1960s.

Born Alexandra Domontovich in 1872 (Kollontai was her married name), she grew up in St. Petersburg, a member of the nobility. Her father was a general in the Russian Army, although not so high ranking as Sofia Perovskaia's; her mother was a landowner. Kollontai's early years were like those of many female revolutionaries of her generation: she moved away from her politically liberal family into a marriage that ultimately proved unsatisfactory and then into the Social-Democratic Party. Unusual only in her personal ambition to write about Marxism rather than work in the revolutionary underground, by 1917 Kollontai was a well-published author on socialist topics, particularly the woman question.

During the revolutionary years 1917 to 1921, Kollontai, who had been a Menshevik until 1915, became a very prominent Bolshevik. She built a reputation as one of the Party's best orators and publicists. She worked to establish the Soviet program for women's emancipation, first as Commissar of Social Welfare and then as head of the Zhenotdel. But her effectiveness as an advocate for women was limited by her ongoing politi-

cal disagreements with the party leadership, Lenin in particular. These came to a head in 1921, when, as a spokesperson for the dissenting group called the Workers' Opposition, she vehemently criticized the Party for being too dictatorial. Her outspokenness cost her the post at the Zhenotdel, and in 1922 she left Soviet Russia for an assignment in the diplomatic corps.

Kollontai thought her exile would be short; it lasted until 1945. At first she continued to write about women's issues, producing her most fully developed analysis of women's emancipation in the early 1920s. As her reputation grew abroad, however, it fell at home. Critics in the Party press, suspicious of her political sympathies and the stress she always laid on women's issues, accused her of being more feminist than Marxist. Stung by the rebuke, Kollontai confined herself after 1926 to diplomacy. Ambassador to Sweden from 1930 to 1945, she played an important part in 1941 and 1944 in the negotiations that ended wars between Finland and the Soviet Union. She retired in 1945, moved to Moscow, and lived there until her death in 1952, several weeks short of her eightieth birthday.

digenous customs of local peoples. This was also true among the hunters and fishers of Siberia, who remained at an even greater distance, physically and culturally, from events in Moscow and St. Petersburg. The great social revolution sweeping Russia was kept at bay, and women attended to their traditional tasks.

Women's Activism

Even the participation of the more liberated women of Moscow or Vladivostok or Riga in riots, strikes, and demonstrations was very much affected by already established customs. Many women joined the dramatic outbursts of mass indignation; fewer joined unions and political parties. Peasant women jubilantly looted and burned manor houses along with their men. In the cities, working-class women continued to vent their anger on empty stores and to hold spontaneous strikes to protest the worsening economic situation. Middle-class women marched as well, but they were more likely than working-class women to be demonstrating as representatives of unions and political parties.

For despite the continuing influence of old ideas, the revolutionary year did bring changes in the patterns of female participation in politics. By the end of the year, hundreds of thousands of women had voted for the first time in elections of local soviets and city dumas, and, in the fall, in the national election of the Constituent Assembly.[6] Women also served as delegates to the soviets and city dumas, and as members of the executive committees of both bodies. There were prominent female leaders in the major political parties. Ariadne Tyrkova and Sofia Panina of the Kadet Party were liberals from the intelligentsia, women with long histories of involvement in feminist and philanthropic causes. Panina briefly held the post of Commissar of Social Welfare in the Provisional Government. Alexandra Kollontai became equally well known in 1917, although for very different reasons: she was a fiery Bolshevik orator who had a persuasive way with crowds. Maria Spiridonova of the SRs was the only woman actually to head a political party in 1917. A strong-willed leader who inspired great devotion in her followers, Spiridonova played an important part in the jockeying for power

---

6 The Constituent Assembly was supposed to write a constitution for Russia. It met in January 1918, but was immediately dismissed by the new Bolshevik government.

that took place among the revolutionary parties throughout the year.

Thousands of other women became involved in a variety of organizations all over Russia in 1917. Unions with a history of female militancy, such as the textile workers' union, were never busier, and increasingly women were elected to union boards as well as to the newly established factory committees. In predominantly male unions, women pressed for greater recognition. Working-class women also organized their own new, female-led trade unions, the best known of which were the laundresses' unions and the unions of soldiers' wives. And in all this bustle of activity, feminists and radical socialists were apt to find themselves pitted against each other in hostile competition for the support of working-class women; for now that women had the vote, the SRs and SDs were out to court and capture them. The result was an unprecedented level of female political activity in all of Russia's major cities and in many lesser ones.

This activism made it clear that women would henceforth be a presence on the political scene, if only as members of the various organizations. Now feminists as well as certain socialists long committed to women's emancipation could argue much more persuasively than in the past that the parties' male leaders should pay attention to issues of particular concern to women, such as pay equity and sexual abuse. Thus the revolutionary climate of 1917 not only brought the Bolshevik Party to power in time, it prepared the way for the Bolshevik program of women's emancipation that followed.

BOLSHEVIKS AND THE PROGRAM FOR WOMEN'S EMANCIPATION

Marxist Theory and Marxist Practice

In late October 1917, the Bolsheviks, led by V. I. Lenin and Lev Trotsky, arrested the ministers of the Provisional Government and declared a new government, to be based on the soviets and administered by a Bolshevik-dominated coalition cabinet (the Council of People's Commissars). With this seizure of power the Russian Revolution entered a new phase, one that would have momentous consequences for the women of the empire. For while all the political parties of the center and left had declared their intention to support women's rights, none had committed itself to a more thoroughgoing program for women's emancipation than the Bolsheviks. And none of the others had a cadre of female members already organized to enact that program.

The Bolsheviks did, however. A dozen or so Bolshevik women had begun trying to build support among working-class women before World War I. This group included Nadezhda Krupskaia, Lenin's wife; her good friend, Inessa Armand, a one-time feminist turned revolutionary; and Konkordia Samoilova, the priest's daughter who had organized the first Woman's Day observances in Russia. In 1917 they began to work closely with Alexandra Kollontai, until 1915 a Menshevik (a moderate as revolutionaries went), then increasingly as the war years passed a staunch supporter of Lenin, whose opposition to the war she greatly admired. Since 1905, Kollontai had been the most ardent champion of women's rights of all the Russian SDs. Klavdia Nikolaeva, the printer from the slums of St. Petersburg whom Kollontai had recruited into the revolutionary movement, also joined the efforts to reach out to working-class women in 1917. These veterans were active throughout the year, speaking to women's groups, publishing their newspaper *Rabotnitsa (Working Woman)*, slogging away at unionizing efforts, and, by the fall of the year, organizing local party subcommittees that specialized in persuading working-class women to support the Bolsheviks. By late October, they were planning a working-women's conference in Petrograd.

The particular reforms that the Bolshevik women advocated were taken directly from the platform on women's emancipation worked out by the German Social Democrats in the 1890s and adopted by the Russian SDs in 1903. They included universal suffrage, equal civil and legal rights for women, full equality of access to education and employment, regulation of working conditions to protect women from conditions injurious to their health (especially their reproductive health), and maternity benefits. The Party also advocated the shifting of housework and child care to publicly financed institutions—laundries, restaurants, and day-care centers. These proposals derived from the Marxist premise that for women to be fully equal members of society, they must be completely freed from economic dependence on men. This required the socializing of domestic labor so that women could work as men's equals outside the home. Once the chains of economic dependency had been broken, then marriage and family life would be radically transformed. Women and men would live communally, entering and leaving intimate relationships as they chose, their children cared for by the members of the commune and by the public child-care system.

In many ways, the Marxist analysis of women's oppression was more powerful than that made by the liberal feminists. Certainly it was more thoroughgoing. It incorporated the feminist advocacy of political rights but was also attentive to the problems women encountered in the workplace and in the home. Marxism's solutions were alluring as well. Marxist theory did not merely advocate that women's inequality and resulting burdens should be abolished; it declared that they would be, as an inevitable part of the process of revolution. By sweeping away capitalism, revolution would destroy the source of women's oppression— the institution of private property. When all people, women and men, owned everything in common, all people, women and men, would be equal, and therefore free. This doctrinal linkage between women's emancipation and the emancipation of the entire society made Marxism powerfully appealing to Russian revolutionary women, and made them less patient than they might have been with feminists who ignored, as they saw it, the fundamental injustices of capitalism.

Marxism also contained a critical weakness in its analysis of women's liberation, however, a weakness easily overlooked by optimistic, enthusiastic revolutionaries in 1917. Marx and Engels asserted that gender inequality, like other forms of injustice, emerged from the evil of private property. Women were unequal because men controlled property; they would become equal when revolution swept private property away. But Marx and his nineteenth-century associates, for all their radical and egalitarian ideas, believed that women would not be prime movers in their own emancipation. How indeed could Marx have thought otherwise? He argued that the revolution would occur when factory workers, most of them men in the nineteenth century, rose up to destroy the capitalists and the politicians, also mostly men. Thereafter the workers would build a socialist new world and in the process of creating common ownership would emancipate everybody, women included. It was not that Marx left women out, as political philosophers usually did, but rather that he cast them as beneficiaries of a historical transformation of power and property conducted by the political actors of his day, that is, by men. The Bolsheviks, whether male or female, failed to appreciate the extent to which Marxism assumed the preeminence of men, but it affected them, before, during, and after the revolution.

Furthermore, for all their professions of commitment to the principle of women's emancipation, the Bolsheviks were profoundly distrustful of real-life peasant and working-class women. Like other revolutionaries, they thought poor women were conservative, religious, and hostile to unions and political parties. Why risk wasting precious resources on them, many Bolsheviks argued before the revolution? Why not focus on male workers, who were not so fearful of radicals and whose organized activity, moreover, held the key to revolution? Most Bolsheviks probably thought it was just as well if men made the revolution and women stayed at home. Later, women would be emancipated in any case.

The female Bolsheviks who wanted to organize the female proletariat countered this powerful combination of prejudice and ideology by arguing that cultivating support among women would enlarge the ranks of those fighting for revolution and thereby bring about the millennium sooner. In 1917, after the revolution began (sparked, as the female Bolsheviks liked to point out, by working-class women), Bolsheviks such as Inessa Armand and Alexandra Kollontai agreed with their male comrades that working-class women were "backward," but explained that this was because women suffered under the dual oppression of capitalism and patriarchalism. Those who would reach them had first to understand their situation, and then craft a message that spoke to women's needs and earned their trust. Won over by sympathetic organizers, women would become important supporters of the revolution and the Bolshevik Party. This argument drew strength in 1917 and thereafter from the unprecedented levels of female activism during the revolution. Encouraged, a group of several dozen Bolsheviks led by Armand and Kollontai set out in the months following the October seizure of power to cultivate support among working-class women and to implement the Party's program for women's emancipation.

First Measures, 1917–1919

From December 1917 to January 1919, the Bolshevik government drafted a series of laws, decrees, and declarations of intent that laid the foundation for the Soviet program of women's emancipation. A new constitution issued in 1918 declared women's full political equality. A family law code drafted the same year proclaimed women's legal equality. It also made marriage a civil procedure (thus removing it from the jurisdiction of the Russian Orthodox Church), legalized divorce, and abolished the discrimination formerly practiced against illegitimate children by granting all children the legal right to parental economic support. The goal of these changes was, in the phrase often used at the time, to make marriage "a free union of equal citizens."

These legal reforms were accompanied by efforts to improve women's position in the labor force. The Commissariat of Labor issued a series of decrees in late 1917 and early 1918 declaring women's rights to employment. It also began mandating pregnancy leave and drafting protective-labor laws, that is, regulations requiring employers not to assign women tasks that would harm their health. (These regulations were finally codified in the Labor Code of 1922.) Meanwhile Alexandra Kollontai, head of the Commissariat of Social Welfare from November 1917 to March 1918, drew up proposals for public funding of maternity and infant medical care and for stipends to feed and clothe newborns. She also began designing the administrative apparatus necessary for a centralized women's health-care system.

Laying the legal and regulatory foundation for women's equality was one aspect of the revolutionary program. Another was attempting to mobilize women to support the Party and the revolution. Here too the female Bolsheviks made progress. In 1918 they organized a series of local conferences in Petrograd and Moscow, and then a national meeting, the First All-Russian Congress of Women Workers and Peasants, in Moscow in November. More than eleven hundred delegates came from all over central Russia, far more than had been expected. Assembled in a grandly columned room that had once been home to the Moscow town council, they voted enthusiastically for resolutions calling for the immediate implementation of the full Marxist program for women's emancipation, including the establishment of women's equality with men in all aspects of public life, the takeover of housework by public institutions, and the abolition of the patriarchal family. They greeted Armand, Kollontai, Samoilova, Nikolaeva, and all the other Bolsheviks with waves of ebullient applause, and declared their determination to return to their homes and revolutionize the women there. Looking down from the dais on this attentive, inspired audience filled with women from the factories, Kollontai and Armand were elated. The great hall where they met was cold from lack of fuel to heat it, the delegates were dressed in kerchiefs and heavy coats, it had been a struggle to find food to feed them all, but the meeting was a triumph.

It was a very limited triumph, however, as Armand and Kollontai knew, for the Bolsheviks were actually not very popular with the great masses of working-class and peasant women. Probably they were less popular in the fall of 1918 than they had been a year earlier. They had made a very disadvantageous peace with Germany in March 1918, and, only a few months later, had taken up arms against a collection of anti-Bolshevik armies commonly known as the Whites. Conscription was reinstituted, this time to fill the ranks of the newly established Red Army. Adrift, the economy continued to deteriorate. Consequently the hardship of poor women's lives increased in the summer and fall of 1918, and some of them blamed the Bolsheviks. Meetings held at the factories to rally support dissolved into shouting matches. Several times in Petrograd in the summer and fall of 1918 groups of women rushed the platform, grabbed the frightened Bolsheviks who had been speaking, and violently threw them out. The Bolsheviks had always believed that working-class women were hostile to them; now, in the fall of 1918, there was ample evidence to support that belief. So the women's congress was both a singular accomplishment and a paradox. Were proletarian women fundamentally hostile? Or were they merely uninformed, a salvageable, untapped resource for a party desperately in need of all the support it could muster?

Armand, Kollontai, Samoilova, and the other Bolsheviks who were increasingly coming to specialize in what they called "work with women" argued that women could be a source of either strength or weakness for the Party. If appealed to in ways that they understood, they would flock to the Bolsheviks, as those delegates had flocked to the All-Russian Congress. If ignored, they might keep up a sullen resistance that could eventually even undermine the Party's reputation among working-class men. Bolstered by the success of the congress, Armand and Kollontai proposed that the Party establish a permanent organization to specialize in enlisting the support of working-class and peasant women. This request was granted in the fall of 1919. Inessa Armand became the head of the new Department for Work Among Women, an agency of the Central Committee of the All-Russian Communist Party. In the fashion of Soviet bureaucracy the Bolsheviks quickly thought up an acronym for the new apparatus—*Zhenotdel*.[7] The Zhenotdel soon became one of the most remarkable organizations in the history of the women's emancipation movement.

Its stated purpose was to conduct "agitation and propaganda" among working-class and peasant women. "Agitation" meant the repetition of simple messages to unsophisticated audiences. Once people had mastered the lessons agitators taught them, then they could move on to the more complex theoretical understanding of Marxism that "propaganda" imparted. In 1919, the Zhenotdel's leaders planned a national campaign of agitation and propaganda to be conducted by a network of organizers operating out of local and regional Party committees. Those organizers would persuade working-class and peasant women to attend conferences where they would study the basics of Marxism, the program on women's emancipation, and the meaning of current events (interpreted, of course, from a Bolshevik perspective). They would also learn what the Party's priorities of the moment were, and what the Party wanted them to do at

---

7 "Zhen" is the first syllable of the Russian word for woman, *zhenshchina; otdel* means "department" or "section."

the local level. Well briefed, the delegates would go back to their factories to teach what they had learned to their female co-workers.

The Zhenotdel leaders harbored other ambitions for the department as well, seeing it not simply as a way to cultivate female support but also as an engine for promoting women's emancipation. Zhenotdel workers throughout the country would train women to build and run day-care centers and medical clinics. They would lobby union boards and factory managers to hire and promote women, to enforce protective-labor regulations, and to set up cafeterias and day-care centers. They would persuade local officials of the Commissariat of Education to hold literacy classes for women. All this would be driven by the additional energy of legions of female factory workers going to delegate conferences and then serving internships in the Health Commissariat or the Commissariat of Labor. Having been trained in administering kindergartens, clinics, and public restaurants, the interns would return to their factories to work in such programs there. And while working-class and peasant women made the revolution at the grass roots, the national Zhenotdel leadership would be lobbying male Party leaders to pay attention to women's issues.

This was a bold agenda for a party struggling desperately to hold power during a brutal civil war. That civil war actually made the Zhenotdel possible, for it created the desperate need for mass support that convinced male Party leaders to establish the department. The war also demanded the male leaders' attention, leaving the Zhenotdel's leaders alone to define their own mission and work out their projects. Yet at the same time, the civil war worsened the hardships against which women struggled throughout Russia and thereby made it ever more difficult for the Zhenotdel to succeed in reaching them.

THE CIVIL WAR

The war that began in 1918 and ended in 1920 (with isolated, sporadic outbreaks for several years thereafter) pitted the Bolshevik-led Red Army against shifting coalitions of anti-Bolshevik forces (the Whites). The Whites attempted to batter their way from the periphery of the old Russian empire (Siberia, Ukraine, the Baltic states) to Moscow; the Red Army fought back from its bases in the Russian heartland. The toll in human life was terrible, not just because of the substantial combat casualties, but because of the huge numbers of civilians who succumbed to disease and famine. The strain of the civil war, piled onto the effects of World War I, caused the collapse of the Russian economy. Food supplies to the cities dropped to starvation levels, forcing mass migrations back to the countryside. In the villages food became scarce as well because of the disruptions of war and several years of bad weather. The result was pervasive malnutrition, which left people more vulnerable to epidemics of typhus, typhoid, influenza, and cholera. Estimates put the total dead as a result of the catastrophic problems of World War I and the civil war at 16 million.

The strategies women adopted to survive the crisis were many, but for purposes of analysis they may be thought of broadly under two categories—the preservation response and the revolutionary response. The former was the more common: women relied primarily on familiar institutions to sustain them. Thus urban women turned to the family to get them through, whether their natal family or their married one, and if they had neither, they tried to construct one by hastily marrying. (The urban marriage rate rose sharply in 1918 and 1919.) They also fled the starving cities by the millions, going back to the villages to live with their kin. The population of Petrograd dropped 72 percent between 1918 and 1920, the population of Moscow by more than 50 percent.

Peasant women also clung to their families and to the village. When Zhenotdel workers ventured into the countryside during the civil war, peasant women often greeted them with suspicion. They knew that the Women's Department had little to offer them but words. Furthermore, they feared that the Bolsheviks' plans to emancipate women (which had filtered through to them as wildly distorted rumors) might disrupt the village still further. And of course they were right. For what was it that women were to be emancipated from, but the society of the village, the other men, women, and children on whom they were relying for survival? It is understandable, therefore, that women often responded to the few Zhenotdel organizers who came among them by turning a deaf ear, or running the strangers out of town.

Their anxiety resulted not just from the dangers of the civil war, but also from the fact that stresses from the earlier war and the revolution had already changed village life in so many ways. Years of upheaval had cut agricultural productivity throughout the empire, as well as increased women's workload. The revolution radicalized millions of peasant soldiers and sent them flooding back from the front. For decades before the war young men who had been to the city had been notably less willing to submit to the authority of the patriarchs than those who stayed at home. Now the revolution emboldened the young more than ever before. When the village elders met to distribute the land they had seized from the landlords in 1917 and 1918, sons demanded the right to shares of their own, so that they could move away from their parents' houses and set up independent households. Often they were urged on by their wives, who were anxious to become their own mistresses. All this change unsettled everyone, and made them more inclined than ever to reject the radical plans brought in by unknown outsiders.

The Bolsheviks took that reaction as yet another indication of the peasantry's notorious backwardness. Once again peasant women were accused of refusing to embrace the revolution that promised them liberation. The truth was that poor women, peasant and working-class alike, relied on traditional defenses to get them through the crisis because traditional institutions were all most of them could rely on. To leave the shelter of those institutions, however intolerable they might be, was to court disasters still more insufferable, and if a woman had children, disaster might be visited upon them as well. Thus when working-class or peasant women spread stories about how the Bolsheviks were devils who wanted to steal everyone's babies, or when they gathered in an angry crowd to defend a church or berate a Zhenotdel worker, they were not simply behaving like mindless conservatives. They were defending traditional institutions because they needed them.

There were women who did answer the Party's call, who made what might be called the revolutionary response, working with the Zhenotdel, joining the Communist Party, and fighting in the civil war. Although a tiny fraction of Russia's female population, the numbers of such women were substantial. Tens of thousands participated in Zhenotdel projects. More than fifty thousand joined the Communist Party during the civil war, most of them young, single city-dwellers of middle-class backgrounds. Sixty-five thousand working-class and middle-class women also volunteered for service in the Red Army.

They worked mostly as nurses, drivers, or clerks—jobs women had filled in the tsarist army in World War I. But the Bolsheviks also employed women (and men) as "political officers" charged with propagandizing the troops and checking on the behavior of the thousands of Red Army officers who were suspect because they had earlier held commissions in the tsarist army. Female political officers worked very near the front, and it was not uncommon for them to take part in combat. Stories circulated of women who rallied troops wavering on the verge of retreat by drawing their revolvers and rushing forward into enemy fire.

Women also served during the civil war in other nontraditional positions. Some worked as spies behind White lines. Women were valuable in such assignments, because they were less likely to fall under suspicion than male infiltrators. There were also female officers in the Cheka, the police agency set up to ferret out the Bolsheviks' enemies. Female judges served on revolutionary courts as well. Word of the harshness of the penalties meted out by these women spread quickly. Varvara Iakovleva, a woman from a merchant family, who had been a revolutionary since 1904, earned the name "Bloody Iakovleva" for her zeal in executing captives. Another Bolshevik of long standing, Rozalia Zemliachka, was removed from her position as political officer in the Crimea in 1920 because of the brutal retributions she had ordered against White sympathizers. Perhaps these women really were particularly ferocious, but it is also likely that their reputations grew from a horrified reaction to women being implicated in the atrocious cruelty of the civil war.

Naturally there was resistance to women moving outside of nursing and other support activities into positions in the military where they exercised authority. Red Army soldiers claimed that women did not belong at the front and gave the reasons given by soldiers everywhere: women disrupted the camaraderie of the men; they had to be taken care of, thus endangering the men; they could not cope emotionally or physically with the demands of war. The men cherished as well a deep opposition to women giving them orders. To drive the women away soldiers harassed them; they sabotaged the women's work, giving them miserable horses to ride, uniforms many sizes too big to wear, or broken-down equipment to work with. Some men took every opportunity to ridicule women, laughing at them when they had difficulties coping with life at the front and refusing to help them. Such men, cursing loudly or telling vulgar stories, ostentatiously displayed the crudeness of their all-male world as a way to shut the women out. Occasionally some particularly hostile soldiers resorted to physical abuse, even rape. Such behavior was not universal; many female veterans reported that the soldiers with whom they worked treated them humanely. But the problems Soviet women sometimes encountered during the civil war were a portent of the sort of resistance they would meet later as they entered other fields that had once fallen within the exclusive preserves of men.

CONCLUSIONS

By 1921 the people of Russia had dismantled the empire of the tsars and attacked much of the structure of everyday life as well. Nicholas II was dead, the nobles had been driven from their manor houses, and a new ruling group was in place with radically new goals for the society. Peasants had attained their long-dreamed-of control over the land. The Church, venerated for centuries, was under siege. The nation's youth were shaking off the control of their elders and defying custom and even the rules of ordinary decorum. Intellectuals were designing new forms of art, architecture, literature, ballet, and symphonic music. Meetings of women were passing resolutions calling for radical changes in family life. In four short years, the world of Old Russia had been turned upside down.

Whether they hailed the revolution or excoriated it, most people agreed that fundamental change had occurred and was still occurring. But people, in their fear or delight, were actually overestimating what the revolution had wrought. The great upheaval brought to fruition some developments long in the making, primarily the collapse of the tsarist political system and the Church. It accelerated others, such as the sons' challenge to the power of peasant elders. And it disseminated ideas concerning women's emancipation that had long been held by the intelligentsia but only fitfully communicated to the masses. It also brought to power two regimes, first the short-lived Provisional Government and then the Bolsheviks, that issued landmark decrees concerning women's emancipation.

Yet women were as divided in their reactions to the revolution and the ferment that produced it as men were. Those who had worked for it welcomed it, and in 1921 had high hopes that a new, just society was in genesis. Others, throughout the country the great majority, had experienced little but misery from all the years of war, and understood only dimly the strange new ideas swirling toward them from the cities. So much change, accompanied by so much hardship, was frightening and unsettling. Once peace returned, a process of consolidation would begin. Elements of the new would be harmonized with elements of the old to produce by the 1930s the Soviet system. The 1920s saw the beginning of this deeper consolidation as well as a dazzling, if more superficial, display of experimentation and change.

3 / BUILDING A NEW ORDER
1921 – 1941

The 1920s were a decade vibrant with the utopian impulses unleashed by the revolution. The twenties were also years when
the processes of modernization that had begun long before the
revolution, particularly those transforming family life, continued
to assert themselves. The Communist Party tried to control this
flood of changes according to its own agenda, but the Party itself
was changing from a prerevolutionary movement run by radical
intellectuals into a bureaucratized government staffed by people
only recently arrived from the villages. How Party members were
going to transform society, and indeed, what they wanted it to
be, were questions they hotly contested throughout the 1920s.
They resolved them by submitting to an increasingly authori-
tarian government which, by the 1930s, was actively promoting
a revised set of social definitions that blended traditional, utopian, and modernizing influences.

Defining the position of women became a central issue in the
creation of the new society. What sorts of work were women to
do? How were they to harmonize their jobs and family lives?
Which of the old ideas about women would be abandoned, and
which preserved? These issues were settled in part by Party fiat,
in part by the habits and attitudes and behavior of millions of
Soviet women. By the end of the 1930s, the complex interplay
of these forces had given birth to the values, norms, and roles
that would structure women's lives throughout the Soviet period, and thereafter.

THE 1920s

Women in the Avant Garde

The 1920s were a time in the newborn Soviet Union when many
people believed that the revolution had removed the hobbles

and blinders of the past, freeing human beings to achieve anything and redefine everything. Young people tried to redesign
the family by living in communes. Architects and engineers drew
up plans for steel and glass cities, marvels of technology where
there would be no poverty or despair. Moviemakers told their
stories with seriousness and intensity and developed new camera
angles and editing techniques that had a powerful impact on
film. Musicians, poets, and writers all crowded forward with new
rhythms and new themes.

Many women took part in all these experiments, particularly
in the arts, for women had been prominent in the literary and
artistic community in Russia before the revolution. Nowhere were
women more numerous than among the painters, sculptors, and
designers known today as the Russian avant garde. Perhaps the
most brilliantly versatile painter was Liubov Popova, who brought
the bright colors of Russian icons to the forms of cubism and
abstractionism. There were many others who worked in oils, in
graphic design, and in the reshaping of everyday objects such
as dishes, clothing, and textiles. Their radically abstract paintings,
collages, and posters broke with all the artistic conventions of
the past, as they sought to shake up art just as the revolution
had shaken up society. They saw themselves not as the hired
hands of the rich, a role artists had usually played in the past,
but rather as servants of the people, working to making products that would brighten and improve their lives. Of course they
were also missionary-propagandists, trying to educate their audience; and the audience, it must be admitted, was not always wildly
receptive. Few Soviet women rushed out to buy cotton cloth
printed all over with tiny tractor drivers or heroic workers stoking
blast furnaces; they preferred flowers. But throughout the 1920s,
the women and men of the avant garde poured out innovative
images and artistic ideas that did indeed brighten and uplift the
Soviet Union's dirty, dishevelled cities. As the government became increasingly intolerant of their experimentation in the later
years of the decade, some emigrated, while others began producing more conventional work. But the bold shapes and stark
lines of their pioneering vision made a lasting impact in the
Soviet Union, and were perhaps even more influential abroad.
This is why today their work—colorful, abstract, ingenious, and
modern—looks so familiar.

The Zhenotdel

The Zhenotdel, or Woman's Department, was the other great contribution women made to the experimentation of the NEP years.[1] Like the avant garde, it succumbed at the end of the decade to government suppression, but while it lasted, the Zhenotdel ran up a remarkable record of achievements. It played a central role in developing the program for women's liberation that was to become the model for communist governments around the world.

The department grew in size from a few staffers in 1919 to an agency employing thousands in the mid-1920s. Its headquarters were in Moscow; branches were established in cities and towns across the Soviet Union. Five women led the department during its eleven-year existence: Inessa Armand (1919–1920), Alexandra Kollontai (1920–1922), Sofia Smidovich (1922–1924), Klavdia Nikolaeva (1924–1925), and Anna Artiukhina (1925–1930). They were typical Old Bolsheviks.[2] Armand, Kollontai, and Smidovich had grown up in gentry families that were politically liberal; they had all attended the university courses for women, then worked in charity projects, and had become revolutionaries when they decided that charity would not solve Russia's problems. Nikolaeva and Artiukhina had taken a similar path from the factories where they worked: they had joined the unions but after a few years came to believe that revolution was Russia's only hope. All five had worked among women before the revolution, and all were deeply committed to the Marxist vision of women's liberation. They were Marxist feminists, for they made reforms for women their main priority. (Of course, they themselves were very critical of feminism and would never have accepted that label.) They gathered around themselves a staff of enthusiastic younger women, at first most of them of middle-class background. Later in the 1920s more women from the working class and peasantry came into the department.

---

1 NEP stands for New Economic Policy, a set of economic reforms initiated in 1921 that permitted some private enterprise. It also refers to the atmosphere of experimentation that prevailed in the 1920s.
2 That is, people who had joined the party before 1917.

It is perhaps regrettable that the Zhenotdel's relationships to the Party leadership on the one hand and to local and regional Party organizations on the other were never adequately defined. It was not clear whether provincial Zhenotdel workers took orders from the local Party committee or from the leadership of their own department. Nor was it clear whether the Zhenotdel itself was an independent agency under the Party's Central Committee, or a branch of the Department of Agitation and Propaganda, from which it received its funding. Such confusion was typical of the early Party bureaucracy, which grew very quickly and haphazardly during the civil war and the early 1920s. But while the lines of command were soon clarified in other cases, the awkward status of the Zhenotdel was never resolved, probably due to the unique ambivalence many communists felt about the department. After all, there was no ideological basis in Marxism for women to claim the right to an independent organization, and certainly no basis for such a claim within the emerging Party structure, which was highly centralized in principle and dependent for everyday functioning on networks of power and patronage among men. The Zhenotdel's uncertain status meant that its leaders were continually obliged to negotiate power and favors from the Party leaders, most of the time winning their support but never quite obtaining from them recognition as an independent agency. Nor could the Zhenotdel heads ever secure what they regarded as sufficient funding or staffing. In consequence they were never able to carry out more than a fraction of their ambitious plans, and indeed their very successes often depended on the work of unpaid volunteers.

In spite of being patched together with hard work and good will (like so many feminist projects in the West), the Zhenotdel pursued its dream of emancipating women. It trumpeted its message by publishing magazines, pamphlets and books, sending organizers out to talk to women in the villages and factory towns where they lived and worked, and holding delegate conferences. The publications were probably the most successful of these undertakings, for they reached an audience of millions and lasted long after the Zhenotdel was gone. By the early 1930s, the department's publication list included hundreds of books and pamphlets, as well as eighteen women's magazines which collectively produced more than 1 million copies per year. The most popular of the magazines were *Krestianka* (*Peasant Woman*) and *Rabotnitsa* (*Woman Worker*). Published monthly, both magazines included short stories, poems, articles on current events, portraits of prominent women, tips on child care, cooking, and hygiene, and even contained clothing patterns. In the 1920s the Zhenotdel staffers who edited them made women's emancipation their central theme. They publicized new opportunities open to women: "Can a Woman Be a Metal Worker?" asked one typical series of articles in 1926 (the answer was yes).[3] To free women from domestic work, they promoted the establishment of daycare centers, public restaurants, and laundries. They also confronted the ongoing problems women faced, taking pointed aim at sexist prejudice in the family and in the workplace and condemning male violence and abuse of women. The editors reached out to their readers by soliciting literary contributions from all over the Soviet Union and by printing some of the thousands of letters they received. Although *Krestianka* and *Rabotnitsa* became much blander after the Zhenotdel was abolished, they continued to be popular for many decades afterwards and remain important as a permanent legacy of the department.

The Zhenotdel got its message out in many other ways. It sent speakers to cities, towns, and villages. Its staffers set up reading rooms in apartment buildings and factories. Zhenotdel workers even read aloud to peasant women at sewing circles on long winter evenings. Such efforts touched the lives of many millions of women in the 1920s. But at the center of this work, as the Zhenotdel leaders saw it, was the pyramidal system of conferences they organized. Such conferences, lasting one or two days and bringing together masses of female delegates elected by working-class and peasant women, furnished an ideal setting not only for inspirational Marxist lectures, but for strengthening the visibility, collective morale, and do-it-yourself spirit of the women's movement, operating as it was on the left flank of the Party. Between 1919 and 1933 (when the last delegate conference met), 10 million women came to such meetings. Many of them went on to work in the internships mentioned earlier, mostly in government departments but, by the later 1920s, in trade unions as well.

---

3 *Rabotnitsa*, no. 8 (1926): 20; no. 11 (1926): 17; no. 13 (1926): 14.

Zhenotdel staffers at the national and local level took part also in the projects of other departments, sometimes moving in to do what was supposed to be handled by others. They ran women's literacy classes. They coordinated classes in prenatal, infant, and child care. They organized workshops for the unemployed, set up training programs to teach women new skills, and sponsored restaurants and day-care centers. Zhenotdel organizers also helped single and widowed peasant women operate cooperatives that sold food at low prices.

The Zhenotdel even assisted a few collective farms that were run exclusively by women, mostly widows who had left their home villages because they were not being treated well there. One such farm, named in honor of Anna Artiukhina, the head of the Zhenotdel, was a fairly large community of several hundred women who worked communally, raised grain and poultry, and lived in a specially built village that included dormitories, a day-care center and school, and a medical clinic. As yet we do not know how many such communes there were, but none seems to have survived the collectivization of agriculture in the 1930s.

The Zhenotdel's leaders always emphasized that working-class and peasant women should run these various projects themselves. Typically, a Zhenotdel worker would come into a factory or village and convince the women who worked there to set up a day-care center or a lunchroom with donated supplies and mostly volunteer labor. It was emancipation on a shoestring, but the Zhenotdel leaders emphasized the value of developing women's independence and initiative. The argument had the ring of truth, even if it was born of necessity. Getting women active in their own workplaces and neighborhoods also helped give the lie to the old idea that women were too ignorant and conservative to do anything on their own.

The suspicion the Bolsheviks had long harbored toward women's organizations continued to dog the department throughout its existence. The Zhenotdel tried for years to send organizers into the trade unions, but had little success because union leaders rejected outside interference. Still greater were the Zhenotdel's problems with the Communist Party's leadership, particularly with low-ranking officials, many of whom wielded considerable power in provincial cities and towns. That leadership was overwhelmingly male; in 1928, for example, women held virtually no Party offices except in the Zhenotdel (though the Party itself was then about 13 percent female).[4] The leadership was supposed to work with the Zhenotdel, and indeed many Party officials did. They gave Zhenotdel staffers office space, let them use the Party's printing services, publicized their work, and advised them. But others, probably the majority, ignored the Zhenotdel, letting its staffers run their projects but not helping them. Worse still, many communists, particularly those on city, neighborhood, and rural Party committees, went farther than neglect. They actively sabotaged the department by assigning its workers to other jobs, banning them from Party offices, even refusing them permission to speak at Party meetings. In fact, throughout the twenties local Party officials petitioned the national leadership to abolish the Zhenotdel altogether. Only the support of the Politburo ensured the department's survival.

There were many reasons why lower-ranking communists resented and refused to help the Zhenotdel. Most of the women who worked for it were very young and very inexperienced. Undoubtedly some of them made mistakes and irritated rather than organized working-class and peasant women. Others, overwhelmed by the gigantic scale of their job and the pitiful meagerness of their resources, were able to accomplish nothing. But male communists were hostile not just because of the Zhenotdel's shortcomings; after all, in the 1920s the Party was full of inexperienced people who were not performing very well. The distrust and hostility also reflected the longstanding feeling that a women's organization was both feminist and a waste of time and money. This prejudice was particularly common among low-ranking communists, many of whom were poorly educated workers or peasants who had joined the Party during the civil war. Sexist attitudes were stronger here than among the older Bolsheviks who in the prerevolutionary years had imbibed the intelligentsia's open-mindedness on the woman question. The

4 In 1928 women were only 3 percent of secretaries of Party cells. No women were secretaries of the higher ranking, more powerful Party committees of the cities or provinces of the U.S.S.R.

younger generation was also more suspicious than its elders of the educated, independent women who led the Zhenotdel.

Without the backing of the national leadership, the Zhenotdel would not have survived the 1920s. That backing, however, came at a price, one that became clearer as the decade proceeded and a new, less sympathetic Party leadership emerged under Joseph Stalin. The Zhenotdel's leaders professed their intention simply to make loyal citizens out of Soviet women by instructing them in their social obligations and coaxing them out of their conservatism. They denied any intention to act as women's representatives, though in fact they often did just that, reminding the Party's leaders of their responsibilities to the female population. As the decade proceeded and a rising Party elite laid the foundations for the Stalinist dictatorship, the demands for conformity from all Party organizations grew ever more insistent. Outwardly, the Zhenotdel followed the current, its periodicals and speakers becoming, more and more, the mouthpieces for the central government. The Zhenotdel's publications became more inclined to laud the achievements of the Party and to blame the difficulties in women's lives on women themselves, rather than on problems in the Soviet system. Probably its leaders privately deplored this turn of events, but direct evidence of their disappointment may not turn up until researchers finish sifting through the newly opened Party archives. There are indications that they muted their feminist message as the twenties passed in the hope that by thus supplicating the male leadership, they would be permitted to continue their work.

Ultimately this strategy failed. The men who rose to power with Stalin in the late 1920s shared the views of those communists who had been dubious about, if not opposed to, the Women's Department ever since the Revolution. Many of them saw no need for a separate women's organization. Thus in the last month of the postrevolutionary decade, December 1929, the Central Committee announced that the Zhenotdel would be abolished. The department had been established to rally women to the revolution and to socialism. This had been accomplished. What purpose could the Zhenotdel possibly serve, now that women by the millions were thronging into the schools and factories all over the Soviet Union? Hereafter, agitation among women would be carried out by Agitprop departments and trade unions, while social services, educational programs, and job training would be taken over by the appropriate government agencies.

The Party's decision was hard to quarrel with. The Zhenotdel had been set up to mobilize women's support, not to be their advocate. Kollontai, Armand, and all the other Zhenotdel workers had pushed well beyond their authorized functions and for a while had made of their department much more than was originally anticipated, at least by the men who had authorized it. But Stalin and his commissars had no intention of permitting any department such leeway, let alone one they thought of questionable worth. Thus they abolished it in a general cleanup of the Party structure that also saw the end to several departments that had specialized in work with various ethnic groups.

While it lasted, the Zhenotdel compiled a remarkable record of achievement. It played a central role in developing and implementing the Party's program of reforms for women. It publicized Marxist feminism among millions of Soviet citizens. It recruited and trained a generation of communist women who went on later to work throughout the Soviet system as teachers, doctors, engineers, administrators, and factory managers. Viewed from another angle, it was also one of the most utopian, most egalitarian, most hopeful ventures of the 1920s. The Zhenotdel was hundreds of young women, some still teenagers, walking barefoot from village to village in the summers, carrying copies of *Krestianka* to read aloud to peasants in the evenings. It was factory workers in kerchiefs proudly opening the day-care centers they had scrounged and saved for. It was communes and cooperatives, lunchrooms and laundries, all organized and run by women. That is, the Zhenotdel was not just an underfunded agency struggling against ultimately insuperable obstacles; it was also, like so much else in the 1920s, a project animated by a magical sense of the limitless possibilities of a revolutionary new world.

Change in the 1920s—Peasant Women

Yet Zhenotdel workers also knew that the nation they were hoping to transform was still poverty stricken and still wedded to ancient beliefs. Nowhere were poverty and tradition more an obstacle to social transformation than in the countryside where the great mass of the population still lived. Despite the turmoil around them, peasant men and women managed to preserve the village throughout the twenties. They continued to live in large, multigenerational families, though there were now more nuclear families than there had been earlier because so many adult children during the civil war had moved away from their parents and into their own houses. The rural birth rate and marriage rate remained high, the divorce rate low.

Most peasant women were still illiterate, devoutly religious, and suspicious of the communists. They still believed that politics was men's business, and remembered the punishment in store for women who overstepped custom's boundaries. Those who came to the polls to vote in Soviet elections were sometimes heckled and cursed. Naturally, many fewer peasant women than men voted. There were also far fewer female officeholders in the countryside than in the cities.

And yet the barriers against change in the countryside had been weakened by the revolution. The female peasant population for the entire Soviet Union was estimated at 64 million in 1928. Some of these women, particularly those who were young and who had received some education, listened eagerly to Zhenotdel organizers and local government officials as they talked about women's rights. Of the 620,000 women who served as delegates to Zhenotdel conferences in 1927, 384,400 (62 percent) were peasants. The number of peasant female voters increased significantly also, going (for example) from 19 percent of eligible women in 1925 to 30 percent just two years later. In addition, more women were now leaving the countryside and moving permanently to the cities. These facts all provide evidence of the growing penetration of the countryside by urban as well as communist values.

This was far less true in non-Slavic areas. Among the peoples of the Caucasus and of Central Asia, traditional society remained stronger than in the Russian heartland. Particularly in Muslim Central Asia, the region divided into the Kazak, Uzbek, Turkmen, Tadzhik, and Kirghiz Soviet Socialist Republics, women continued during most of the twenties to live much as they had for centuries, tending the flocks, growing grapes and apples, weaving bright cloth, and nursing babies. The revolution did not affect Central Asia's women very much until a concerted effort to emancipate them led to disaster.

It began with the good intentions of the Zhenotdel. The Zhenotdel's leaders, horrified by the power Muslim men wielded over women, sought to include Muslim women in all their national conferences and campaigns from the earliest days of the department. They could achieve little, however, until the mid-twenties, when the Red Army finally broke the resistance to Moscow's rule that had lingered in the mountains of Central Asia. Then the Party leadership began to plan its campaign against the traditional culture that had inspired the resistance. At this point Anna Artiukhina, the outspoken textile worker from St. Petersburg who served as head of the Zhenotdel from 1925 to 1930, convinced her male comrades that the best way to weaken both tradition and Islam was to reach out to the most downtrodden elements in Muslim society, that is, the women. Central Asia was a bulwark of both tradition and Islam. It was chosen as the test case, and Artiukhina volunteered the Zhenotdel to lead one wing of the assault.

With full Party backing, Zhenotdel workers fanned out across Central Asia in 1926 and 1927, preaching their message of women's liberation. They managed to persuade small groups of local women to come to public meetings and take off their veils, symbolically repudiating their subordination. Newspapers carried pictures of Muslim women walking bravely through unfriendly crowds, and Zhenotdel organizers cabled news of their successes to a delighted Artiukhina back in Moscow. But soon these small victories brought forth a spreading calamity. Outraged men fought back against the attack on their power and their world with vigilante violence. Women who had attended the meetings were beaten and even killed by angry husbands and fathers. Zhenotdel staffers were waylaid on the roads at night and murdered. At the peak of the upheaval in 1928, gangs rampaged through the cities and towns of Central Asia, raping and murdering local women and Zhenotdel workers, and assaulting some of the communist officials who had supported them. The violence flared and subsided, then flared up again for almost two years. The government struck back with all the police it could muster and even with troops. By the time it regained control in 1929, more than 800 people, most of them women, had been slaughtered. Artiukhina took the violence as yet more evidence of the dreadful backwardness of Muslim men, but she could not justify fighting it at such heavy costs. Appalled at the disaster, Moscow thereafter adopted a much more cautious approach to the emancipation of Muslim women.

Thus in the 1920s the traditionalism of the countryside continued to assert itself. In Slavic lands, where modernization had already begun to make inroads into the villages before the revolution, change continued. In other areas, where patriarchal institutions had scarcely been challenged before 1917, resistance was fierce. Everywhere, the cities remained the place where utopian experiments flourished and where women's lives were changing most rapidly.

Change in the 1920s—Urban Women

City life was hard in the 1920s, but it could also be exciting, particularly in major centers such as Moscow, St. Petersburg, and Kiev. With the end of the civil war, the cities swelled again with people, especially with women. Many came to rejoin their husbands, but many others were young and single, hunting for the better-paying jobs and greater freedom of the towns. All the essentials of urban life—housing, transportation, consumer goods—remained poor in quality and insufficient in quantity to meet the needs of the growing population, but Soviet cities knew some amenities. There were movies, magazines, newspapers, restaurants, parks, theater, radio, and the circus, even in Siberian outposts such as Irkutsk. Painters, writers, actors, and filmmakers brightened the artistic scene with strange new pictures and dazzling new ideas. Moscow and Leningrad might have seemed drab by comparison with Paris and New York, but they shone brightly enough to peasants up from villages like Temnikov and Staraia Griaznaia.

The cities were also places where women's lives took on the forms that would characterize them subsequently throughout the Soviet period. The greatest changes occurred in the mode and condition of their work, for many women not only entered the waged-labor force in the 1920s but also moved up to better jobs than in the past. The government was responsible for much of this progress. It expanded education for women, providing primary and secondary schooling and job-training programs. It encouraged women to enter fields previously closed to them, particularly skilled manual labor and the professions. And it kept up a drumbeat of propaganda, pounding home the message in the press, in public lectures, and in inner-government communiques, that women were now equal to men and should be educated and employed. All this translated into higher incomes: before the revolution, women in general had earned less than half of what men earned; by 1930 their pay had risen to approximately two-thirds that of men.

Women still had problems in the workplace because male employers continued to harbor many of the old prejudices against female workers, and to discriminate against them. For instance, in the early 1920s when millions of men were demobilized from the army at the same time that the economy was being converted from military to peacetime production, high unemployment resulted, and more women were laid off than men. In part this was because many Soviet people shared the belief, common among Europeans after World War I, that veterans should receive preferential treatment in postwar hiring. But Soviet managers also gave other reasons for laying women off: women, they alleged, were less competent and reliable; they took more time off; they were more expensive employees because of the costs of enforcing protective labor regulations and granting them maternity leave.

To its credit, the government reacted by condemning managers for discriminating against women. Soviet economists produced studies demonstrating that females were every bit as productive and reliable as male workers (who, they drily pointed out, took a great deal of time off to nurse hangovers). The government also soft-pedalled the enforcement of protective labor laws in an effort to cut the costs of employing women, and tried to provide additional relief by encouraging women to seek job training and register with unemployment offices. None of this helped much, however. Female joblessness disappeared only in the enormous expansion of the labor force that came with the First Five-Year Plan of industrial development (1928–1932). Job discrimination did not.

Women's role in the political system also assumed the form in the 1920s that it would take for the rest of Soviet history. Many women, as we have seen, joined mass organizations, and by the mid-twenties urban women, unlike the peasants, were voting in the same percentages as men. Power, however, remained in male hands. Women made up about 20 percent of delegates to the city soviets but held only 10 percent of seats on the soviets' governing executive committees. Ten percent of the members of trade-union factory committees were women, but less than 7 percent of the higher-ranking members of trade-union governing boards were. At the center of power, in the Communist Party, women made up about 15 percent of the membership by the mid-1920s, but as we have seen, only a tiny handful held positions of national prominence. This pattern was not unique to the U.S.S.R. The inauguration of women's suffrage after World War I had not led immediately to their sharing power with men anywhere in Europe or North America. Comparatively speaking, women of the European nationalities in the Soviet Union had made far greater strides in political participation in a shorter period of time than had women elsewhere.

Change in Soviet cities in the 1920s was also affecting the family. Most people now lived in small nuclear families. Despite the birthrate recovery from its precipitous decline during the war years, the typical urban couple had fewer children than its peasant counterpart. This was partly because people were deliberately limiting the size of their families by practicing abstinence and also abortion. (In 1920 the government had reluctantly legalized abortion to protect women from the dangers of illegal operations.) But the size of the family also shrank because of skyrocketing divorce rates in the cities and rising family instability. In the late 1920s Soviet urbanites were divorcing at a higher rate than any other population on earth.

The new patterns of family life in the cities reflected the fact that the rules governing relations between women and men were evolving very quickly. Urban people from all walks of life had begun to idealize and accept romantic love as the proper basis for marriage, thus abandoning the arranged marriages that prevailed among the peasantry. They were having fewer children and lavishing more care and attention on those they had, sending them to school rather than into the fields to work. And they were exercising the right to end their marriages when they chose. Of course, within the new nuclear family, patriarchal customs did persist; women did most of the domestic work and men claimed the right to be the dominant member of the family. But the Party and the schools taught a higher standard of behavior for husbands, condemning men for beating their wives and children and enjoining them instead to treat their loved ones with gentleness and consideration.

All of these changes meant that the modern, nuclear family was replacing the patriarchal, extended one in the Soviet Union, just as it was throughout the industrialized world. Many Soviet citizens feared, however, that the family was not simply changing but disintegrating. There was some evidence to justify their anxiety. Years of war and revolution had shattered thousands of families, leaving an estimated 6 million orphaned, homeless children roaming the cities in the 1920s. Divorced and widowed women struggled to feed their children on their own wages, without support from the extended families they had left behind in the villages or from their departed husbands. Radical new ideas about communal living and free love swirled through student dormitories and factory lunchrooms. Young men, released from priestly and parental controls, were tempted now to see their sexual conquests as affirmations of revolutionary freedom. Thus all the ancient truths about sexuality, love, and parenthood, truths that people had believed since childhood and had clung to through war and revolution, seemed to be at risk.

For many women and children, the situation was simply terrible. Before the 1920s, there had been very few single women in Russia; suddenly millions were widowed or divorced. Urban women, bearing the brunt of contemporary unemployment, had as much reason as before—indeed, more—to rely on marriage for survival. Many were appalled, therefore, by what they perceived as men's increasingly irresponsible, even predatory, behavior. Women from all ranks of society charged that men were taking advantage of the new freedoms to pressure them into sexual relationships and then abandon them to cope with the consequences. Reports of rampant male self-indulgence upset the Party leaders, too, for they had expected the revolution to inspire men to build a new society, not unleash their appetites and detach them from common decency and commitment.

These concerns of ordinary people and of the Party leaders coalesced around two issues: sexual morality and a rewriting of the 1918 marriage law. The consensus that eventually emerged from the debates over these issues was part of a process of defining society's rules in the wake of years of upheaval and revolutionary change, of coming to terms with all that the revolution had unleashed in order to lay the foundations for an orderly new world. The desire to establish boundaries countered the utopians' effort to push beyond limits and quickly proved to be even more popular and influential.

Consolidation in Response to Change

At first glance, both the revision of the marriage law and the establishment of a sexual code for young communists would seem to have been simple enough matters. Throughout the early 1920s women complained that the no-fault divorce law of 1918 made it very difficult for them to collect child support from the fathers of their children. Court procedures were expensive and time-consuming, and the legal system itself frightened many women who were unused to dealing on their own with public institutions. But in a society where so many women were unemployed, where those with jobs still worked for lower wages than men, and where mothers were usually left to rear the children when marriages dissolved, many women felt that they must have stronger legal protection against desertion. Julia Zaitseva, a housewife and wife of a factory worker, put it this way in 1926: "In most cases a woman is more backward and has fewer skills, and therefore she is less independent than a man. For a woman marriage is often the only way 'to define herself.' To get married, to have children, to become enslaved to the kitchen, and then to be thrown out by a man—it's very hard for a woman. So that's why I too am against easy divorce."[5]

The government responded by issuing a new marriage law in 1926 that more clearly defined women's rights to alimony and

------

5 *Rabotnitsa*, no. 15 (1926): 16.

PRASKOVIA ANGELINA

Praskovia Angelina, better known by her nickname Pasha, became a celebrity in the Soviet Union while still a teenager. Born in a village in Ukraine in 1913, Pasha was a student when she first heard the appeals from the government for women to become tractor drivers. Her neighbors said that women were too stupid to do such work, but Pasha ignored them and signed up for one of the first courses open to women. After graduating in the spring of 1930, she found a job at a machine tractor station near her home. That summer Pasha Angelina plowed more land than anyone else working at the station. After the harvest, her boss offered to make her a clerk in the station office, probably because other drivers had complained that she was setting a standard that would humiliate, or exhaust, them all. Angelina refused, geared up her tractor the following spring, and again set records.

This was the beginning of a very famous career. In 1933 Angelina organized an all-female brigade of tractor drivers, and these women in turn trained others. By the mid-1930s she and her team had become some of the Soviet Union's best-known heroines. The press, anxious to encourage more women to take up the work, made media stars out of them; Angelina was even invited to the Kremlin to receive an award from Stalin himself. In 1937 she joined the Communist Party; in 1940 she graduated from a program of agricultural courses at the Timiriazev Academy in Moscow. She spent World War II with her brigade plowing in Kazakhstan, then returned to Ukraine after the war. In the 1950s she was several times elected a delegate to the Supreme Soviet as well as to Party congresses; she also received many medals.

Celebrity did not make Angelina's life an easy one. Tractor-driving was dirty, physically demanding work. For much of her career she battled hostility from her neighbors, female as well as male, who shouted at her that women did not belong on tractors. When she persisted, they spread rumors that she was sleeping with her male co-workers. Her marriage broke up over her husband's demands that she spend more time at home. Nor was the government much more supportive; Angelina's pleas for an expansion of daycare centers and other benefits for women in the countryside generally fell on deaf ears. Few women were persuaded by her example to take up tractor-driving, and by the 1950s she was leading an all-male work crew. Pasha Angelina died of kidney disease in 1959, at the age of 46.

child support and extended those rights to the millions who were living with men they had never legally married.

The sexuality debate occurred at about the same time and centered on the same themes—female economic dependence and male irresponsibility. In the early twenties there were many complaints that young men were enthusiastically preaching and practicing what they called free love. The complaints were lodged most often by young female students and middle-aged male Communists. The young women maintained that love could never be free, particularly for women who had to cope with the pregnancies that resulted. Communist Party elders agreed, preaching sternly to their juniors about the evils of promiscuity throughout the decade. They declared that young men should spend their energies on socially beneficial activities such as education and job training, rather than dissipate them in sexual gymnastics. Furthermore, they charged, the revolution had not freed men to abuse women and then to justify their conduct by proclaiming that monogamy was restrictive and bourgeois. By the late 1920s the Party leaders had come out forthrightly in favor of a sexual code that prescribed premarital chastity and monogamy.

By doing so they embraced standards prevalent in most Western, capitalist nations. They endorsed heterosexual marriage and underwrote the mutual economic and emotional obligations it entailed. Marx and Engels would have disagreed with this rather conventional morality; they had believed, as did most nineteenth-century socialists, that people should run their private lives without being policed by either the government or their neighbors. Marriage would become whatever people wanted it to be, and would end whenever they wanted it to end. Children would be taken care of by communal institutions. This was the thinking that had inspired the 1918 marriage law. This was a spirit appropriate to the utopian civil war years, when communists rejoiced that the old world was falling apart. And it was the spirit that enlivened the more experimental youths of the 1920s. But as the decade drew on, the Party turned from dancing on the ruins of the old world to building a new one. Then the individualistic freedom that Marx had seen as the hallmark of socialism no longer appealed quite so much as did the idea of establishing a new set of rules for a new society, made and enforced by the communist government. Rule-making seemed particularly necessary because so much was shattered by the years of upheaval. In reordering their priorities, the communists enjoyed considerable support from the public, and particularly from the many women who called on the government to protect them from victimization.

The government took up that task almost eagerly, and by the end of the decade the new leaders around Stalin were reaching out to define and control everything in Soviet society. They could, from women's point of view, be powerful allies, able to achieve improvements in short order, as evidenced by the expansion of women's educational and job opportunities in the 1920s. Indeed government has played a crucial role in guaranteeing rights and opportunities for women all over the European world in the twentieth century. The problem was that the Soviet government was an all-male dictatorship that could decide without consultation which aspects of women's emancipation to advance, and which to jettison. In the early 1920s it was still strongly influenced by Marxist feminism; it listened to women's voices and pursued a humane, liberationist agenda. But by the late 1920s this was changing; a new, more autocratic, less tolerant breed of communist came to power. In 1930 these men not only sternly affirmed the obligations of married men, they also abolished the Zhenotdel. Thereafter, the full benefits and costs of dependence on such a power became apparent.

THE 1930s

Mobilizing Women—Industrialization and Collectivization

The Stalin era in Soviet history began in 1928. By that year, Stalin had consolidated his power by discrediting and then removing from office the men who had been the Party's top leaders under Lenin. He then launched two massive initiatives to industrialize the Soviet Union. The First Five-Year Plan (1928–1932) laid out a comprehensive scheme for rapid economic growth. Collectivization of agriculture, although it began in 1929 as an emergency measure to increase grain procurement from the peasants, quickly led to the establishment of direct government control over all farming. Taken together, collectivized agriculture and centralized industrial management became the twin economic bases of Soviet socialism. Both had momentous consequences for women.

Collectivization was more than a governmental takeover of farming. It was a wholesale assault on the village that finally broke the peasants' resistance to the communists. Those peasants who refused to submit to the will of Party-appointed farm managers were threatened, moved off their lands, arrested, and, in some cases, shot. Many retaliated by destroying tools and livestock rather than turning them over to the authorities. The government kept up grain deliveries to the cities, and when the peasants began to go hungry in the early 1930s, the government let them starve. Millions of people perished, and much of the old structure of village life died with them.

Collectivization was an unmitigated personal disaster for millions of peasant women, but it yielded a few meager benefits. The government was eager to court women's support in the 1930s, for planners in Moscow believed that downtrodden peasant women were more likely than men to welcome collectivization, especially if they benefitted from it. This was a variant on the reasoning they had applied to Central Asia, where it had been hoped that improvement in women's lives would promote more general transformation. So women were urged to attend schools and job-training programs newly established in the countryside. They responded quickly, and by the end of the 1930s, literacy among peasant females of European nationality under the age of fifty had risen to 80 percent. Increases were even greater proportionately among the women of the Caucasus and Central Asia. The government also tried to move women into more skilled occupations such as tractor-driving and to employ them as managers on the state and collective farms.[6] Here too there was some success; between 1930 and 1938 the number of female tractor drivers rose from several thousand to

_____

6 State farms (*sovkhozy*) were run like factories; equipment belonged to the government, and the workers were paid regular wages. Collective farms (*kolkhozy*) were designed to resemble the old peasant commune, that is, peasants worked together and were paid with a share of the crop at the end of the season. Machine tractor stations provided heavy equipment to the *kolkhozy*. In practice, both types of farms were run by managers following government plans.

57,500. These women then became media heroines, their exploits featured in newspapers and magazines throughout the Soviet Union. The government also favored women when choosing peasant Stakhanovites, workers who were rewarded for high productivity with handsome bonuses.

But a few years of publicity campaigns and training programs, however well intentioned and attractively packaged, could never overcome the enormous power of peasant beliefs about men and women, or transform ancient convictions about who should lead and who should follow. By the end of the thirties, peasant men, having resigned themselves to the collectivized system, had gone on almost as a matter of right to take over the better-paying jobs of running machinery and managing the farms. The great majority of women were still trudging out to do the most gruelling manual labor, particularly the tending of livestock and the gleaning and gathering that had been considered women's work since time immemorial. This was, of course, a further development of the process that had begun in the nineteenth century, when peasant men took the most desirable work offered by industrialization and rebuffed women who tried to join them. Now, in the thirties, peasant women who learned how to operate machinery—the much-publicized tractor drivers for example—were harassed to the point that many of them quit in despair. Men also assumed the positions that conferred power and authority; by the end of the 1930s, women constituted 57 percent of farm workers, but men occupied 97 percent of the managerial jobs in Soviet agriculture. Collectivization all but destroyed the power of the elders over junior men in the villages, but it did no more than challenge the power of men over women.

The Five-Year Plans bore more positive results for urban women because patriarchy was weaker in the cities. Party planners realized that women were a great untapped labor pool from which to draw the workers needed to build Soviet industry, so they expanded training programs and set quotas for female recruitment. The media kept up a chorus of calls for women to join the great campaign to build industry and socialism and liberate themselves in the process. The schools taught girls to prepare for new sorts of work. The results were gratifying: between 1932 and 1937 women made up 82 percent of all workers entering the paid labor force for the first time. By the end of the decade, they constituted 39 percent of the nonagricultural labor force. They flooded into the fields that had been opened to them in the 1920s, from skilled manual labor to the professions. They flooded as well into the schools as students, so that by the end of the decade 19 percent of urban women in the Soviet Union had finished high school (as compared with 3.5 percent of rural women). Thus at the same time that economic depression was gripping the United States and Western Europe, and female workers there were being laid off in huge numbers, the women of the U.S.S.R., in Siberia and the Caucasus as well as Ukraine and central Russia, were setting records in education and employment.

For all their considerable successes, the Five-Year Plans did not bring about women's liberation because they emphasized the development of heavy industry at the expense of social services and the consumer-goods sector of the economy. The planners argued that heavy industry would produce the forges, drill presses, trams, and trucks that were the basis of a high standard of living. Heavy industry also provided the military equipment to maintain Soviet defenses, a compelling necessity as Adolf Hitler rearmed Germany in the mid-1930s. But the consequence of all this was that funding for consumer goods and basic urban services expanded more slowly than the needs of the growing urban population. As a result, most people coped with squalid housing and difficult conditions at work. Women, bearing the primary responsibility for housework and child care, spent their days at their jobs and their evenings shopping, cooking, and cleaning. The Soviets soon labelled this the "double shift"; women were doing two jobs. Their workload discouraged many from pursuing higher-status, more remunerative careers; they simply did not have the time. Studies from the 1920s and 1930s showed that women on average also slept less than men because of their domestic responsibilities. Thus the warning of Marxism's founding fathers, that women could not be fully equal members of society so long as they did housework, was borne out in the new Marxist state.

Soviet economists acknowledged that this state of affairs was undesirable. They did not admit, however, that the work women did in the second half of their double shift supported the Five-

Year Plans. The more women did, the less had to be spent on day-care centers, restaurants, and laundries. Women's domestic labor has contributed critically to economic growth ever since industrialization began. Housework and child care are real work, essential to the welfare and reproduction of the labor force, but those who perform such work have done it for virtually no financial reward in the Soviet Union as elsewhere. Women's unpaid domestic labor was particularly appealing to Soviet economists and political leaders because they possessed such limited resources and wanted to industrialize so quickly. They did not openly renounce their promise to socialize housework; they just explained that it would take time. For the present, they spent a little more on day-care centers and restaurants—though not enough to meet the demand.

Yet even while they gave lip service to the Marxist principle that housework should be abolished, Soviet leaders were actually adopting new attitudes toward women's domestic roles. They had economic motives to continue the double shift. Increasingly they were discovering social and political ones as well.

The New Soviet Woman

The new attitudes that Stalin's government took toward women and their roles in the family appeared in the mid-1930s in the government-controlled mass media—newspapers, magazines, books, radio, and movies—as well as in various civic activities. In all these venues, the Party promoted conceptions of the ideal Soviet woman. This "New Soviet Woman" differed much from the independent woman envisioned by the Zhenotdel, for far from being liberated from domestic responsibilities, the New Soviet Woman was enamored of them. She was still to be man's equal in the workplace but she was also to devote herself to being his helpmate in their home. In the words of a novel published in 1936, "A wife should . . . be a happy mother and create a serene home atmosphere, without, however, abandoning work for the common welfare. She should know how to combine all these things while matching her husband's performance on the job."[7] This Superwoman—equal citizen, full-time worker, and house-

---

7 From F. Panferov's *The Village Bruski*, quoted by Xenia Gasiorowska, *Women in Soviet Fiction, 1917-67* (Madison, 1968), 53.

wife—appeared in novels, short stories, and movies, where she was portrayed happily attending to her job and her family. Meanwhile the press also publicized the domestic successes of real Soviet women. The wives of Stakhanovites (model workers who exceeded production quotas) were lauded for providing their husbands with moral support and comfortable homes. Wives of engineers came together in conferences where they discussed beautifying the cities their husbands were building. Thus even while promising to do away with housework in the future, the government enjoined women to attend to it now, and to consider creating a happy home an important part of their lives. It did not prescribe such a division of love and labor for the New Soviet Man.

This was unfair, and many communists knew it. After all, before they were silenced, the Zhenotdel activists had pointed out repeatedly that the achievement of socialism itself depended on women's emancipation from the burdens and gender distinctions integral to both traditional and modern family life. Inessa Armand had declared in 1918: "As long as . . . the old forms of the family, home life, and childrearing are not abolished, it will be impossible to destroy exploitation and enslavement, it will be impossible to build socialism."[8] Now in the 1930s the Party was turning its back on these basic Marxist principles and adopting instead contemporary ideas about women's domestic functions that were widely held elsewhere in the European world.

Why did such a thing happen? The problem is complicated. In the first place, the New Soviet Woman appealed to ordinary women throughout the Soviet Union. The great majority of them, Russians in Moscow as well as Kazakhs in Central Asia, had never been communists, had never imbibed the individualism and egalitarianism of Marxist feminism; they still believed that they should tend to their families. They still drew great satisfaction and comfort from mothering, as they had done for centuries, as women have always done. But they did not like being beaten, abused, and abandoned by their husbands and scorned

---

8 Inessa Armand, "Zadachi rabotnits v Sovetskoi Rossii," *Kommunisticheskaia partiia i organizatsiia rabotnits* (Moscow, 1920), 41.

as stupid by the government and the society, as they had been so often in the past. For these women, the New Soviet Woman was an upgrade. She was an equal participant in the society, but she was also securely connected to her family, honored for the loving attention she gave them, and protected by the society. Klavdia Nikolaeva, former head of the Zhenotdel, wrote this description in 1940: "In the Soviet Union woman is active in politics and government and at the same time is a mother, whom our Party and government take care of."[9]

Thus the New Soviet Woman grew, in part, out of beliefs and hopes widespread among millions of Soviet women. She was created, however, not by factory workers or peasants, but by the new Soviet elite of managers and Party officials. Seen from their position in society, the New Soviet Woman was a symbol of status and achievement. Among communists in the 1930s, a happy home life presided over by an accomplished wife signified personal success and material comfort, as it did for people everywhere in the modern world. Those women who came closest to this ideal were the wives of high-ranking communists, who dressed well, lived in special apartment blocks set aside for the rulers, and vacationed at equally exclusive hotels and country homes. Many hired young peasant women to help them with housework and child care. They also could afford to buy the few consumer goods showing up in the shops from time to time. Of course, compared to the luxuries of Western Europe or North America, these Soviet amenities were pathetically shabby. But in the thirties in Moscow, the women who had them stood out. There was no conspicuous consumption; the luxuries, such as they were, were carefully kept behind locked apartment doors, and the newspapers were filled with pictures of female tractor drivers, not fur-coated wives of Party chiefs. But ordinary people could see the elite on the street, could feel their power over their daily lives and understood the status that the real new Soviet women had achieved.

So the idealized New Soviet Woman served the interests and purposes of the elite. Her domesticity signified the status of a

---

9 K. Nikolaeva, I. Karaseva, *Zhenshchina v boiakh za kommunizm* (Moscow, 1940), 7.

new ruling group, but it also provided valuable economic and social services to the society. Her housework and child care meant lower expenditures for social services. The family she anchored would be the cornerstone of social order and of state power, for the husband and children she civilized through her ministrations would be productive, obedient members of society.

Nor would anyone still loyal to Marxist feminism object, since the government had clapped controls on public expression that silenced all dissident voices. Former Zhenotdel workers, including that most ardent Bolshevik feminist Alexandra Kollontai, fell in line and held their peace, if they did not openly endorse the New Soviet Woman, as Nikolaeva did. Independent feminist voices would not be heard again in the Soviet Union until the 1980s.

The endorsement of feminine domesticity received institutional expression in two important legal documents issued in 1936. Yet another draft of the marriage law made divorce more difficult by setting a fee schedule and also by increasing child-support payments and penalties for nonpayment. Abortion became outlawed altogether in an effort to raise the birthrate. People soon learned to circumvent the barriers to divorce simply by separating, and as women in the cities devised a network of illegal abortionists after a year or so, the birthrate remained relatively low. The regulations of 1936, however inefficacious in affecting the actual day-to-day behavior of Soviet citizens, added to the chorus of official endorsements of the nuclear family as the basis of an orderly, productive society.

The Terror

The 1930s were a time of great achievement in the U.S.S.R., and many of the achievers were female. Women moved into and up in the labor force. They graduated from the universities in record numbers and pursued careers in the professions that they could never have aspired to under the tsars. For many such women the decade was a time when the utopian promises of the 1920s seemed to be coming true. But the 1930s were also a decade of horrible persecutions in which millions of Soviet people died at the hands of the very government that had promoted the fortunes of so many of them.

Stalin's regime used violent force willingly and continually, against peasants accused of resisting collectivization, former members of outlawed political parties, priests and the faithful of various denominations, returned POWs, artists and intellectuals, individuals of no suspect category who were simply chosen randomly or reported to the police by avaricious neighbors. The national police charged with investigating political crimes, the NKVD,[10] arrested millions of people from all regions of the Soviet Union during its thirty-year reign of terror.

As yet there are no systematic studies of how the political persecutions of the Stalin years affected women as a distinct group, but it appears that this Terror was primarily a slaughter of men by men, in which women became involved largely by their proximity to men swept up in it. The organizers and enforcers of the Terror—Stalin and his lieutenants, the commanders of the NKVD, the NKVD interrogators, the upper ranks of prison administrators—were all men. The highest ranking women involved in prosecution of the Terror were the guards and wardens in the prisons and camps who supervised female prisoners. Men also made up the great majority of those arrested, then executed or sent to forced labor. There is some evidence that female communists were arrested in numbers proportionate to their membership in the Party, but probably those who fell into the net did so because they were related to men under arrest.

Millions of women suffered terribly from having their husbands, fathers, and sons taken away. One was Anna Akhmatova, the great Russian poet whose son was arrested in 1937. Akhmatova captured women's suffering in her poetry cycle, *Requiem*, recording in one poem the look of those who waited at prison doors for news of their loved ones:

> I have learned how faces fall to bone,
> How under the eyelids terror lurks,
> How suffering inscribes on cheeks
> The hard lines of its cuneiform texts,
> How glossy black or ash-fair locks
> Turn overnight to tarnished silver,

---

10 People's Commissariat for Internal Affairs.

How smiles fade on submissive lips,
And fear quavers in a dry titter.[11]

Often the prison authorities refused to tell these terrified supplicants what had happened to their relatives and prevented communication with them. But the loss of loved ones was only the beginning of a survivor's difficulties. Women also had to make do without their husbands' and fathers' income. Carrying the stigma of being the relative of an "enemy of the people," they found it difficult to hold jobs or complete their educations. Wives were encouraged to divorce arrested husbands, and many did so in order to protect themselves and their children from discrimination.

The women who were arrested entered a horror yet more unimaginable. They lived for months in filthy, cold prison cells and subsisted on starvation rations. NKVD officers subjected women as well as men to "interrogations" that were in effect torture sessions designed to make them confess to crimes they had not committed and to implicate friends and acquaintances. Refusal to cooperate was punished by around-the-clock questioning and solitary confinement. Women were also subjected to sexual abuse.

Until the contents of the archives have been thoroughly studied, we will not know how the police chose whom they would execute and whom they would send instead to the camps. We do know that Stalin and his closest advisers made such decisions in the case of well-known Old Bolsheviks. Viacheslav Molotov, the Chairman of the Council of People's Commissars in the 1930s, admitted much later that he had personally condemned to death the wife of a Communist Party official.[12] How many women were executed during the Stalin era is unknown, but there are reasons to believe that their numbers ran into the tens of thousands. Many appear to have been killed during the peak period of arrests (1936 to 1939) and in the summer of 1941. The bodies of women have been found with men in mass graves in Ukraine, Belorussia, and even Moscow, fully dressed, some still

---

11 Anna Akhmatova, "Requiem 1935–1940," *Poems of Akhmatova*, trans. and ed. by Stanley Kunitz with Max Hayward (Boston, 1973), 113.
12 Feliks Chuev, *Sto sorok besed s Molotovym* (Moscow, 1991), 415.

clutching their purses, killed by a shot to the back of the head and then piled layer on layer into long narrow trenches.

Most female prisoners were not shot but rather were shipped by train to the forced-labor camps, mostly in Siberia, known collectively now by the acronym GULAG (standing for State Camp Administration). Male and female prisoners usually lived in separate compounds, although occasionally they would see one another through the barbed-wire fences. They worked at chopping down trees, building roads, canals, and power plants, and mining gold. They slaved long hours outdoors through the winter in lightly padded jackets and felt boots. Work rules gave them time off only when the temperature fell below minus 50 degrees. They did all this on a meager diet of cabbage soup, black bread, and buckwheat gruel. Millions died. Some survivors were released from this horror in the late 1940s, when their ten-year terms ended, but many more received extensions of their sentences and lived on in the camps until they were amnestied after Stalin's death in 1953.

Evgenia Ginzburg, one of the greatest of the memoirists of the GULAG, wrote that women endured the camps better than men did. She attributed this to the fact that women made strong friendships with one another, whereas men lived more isolated lives and preyed more upon one another. Whether this was generally true cannot be known without further research, but it is intriguing that survivors of the Nazi Holocaust perceived the same differences in men's and women's behavior. In the Soviet camps women may have lived longer also because they were spared the most arduous jobs such as gold mining. Perhaps women adjusted better to imprisonment because they were more accustomed to submission than men. If so, then the inheritance of patriarchal values may have had the unintended benefit of sparing some women from the full consequences of the Terror.

CONCLUSIONS

By 1941 the patterns of women's lives under the Soviet system had been formed. Their status in the society had risen much from the prerevolutionary days, and they had made tremendous gains in education and employment. Their medical care had improved, and the state now recognized its responsibilities towards them and their children. On the other hand, modernization meant the further decline of the various support structures that earlier had existed in the extended patriarchal family. Women had been proclaimed free, but their rights and opportunities were now underwritten by an autocratic government that insisted on subordinating their welfare to its own set of priorities. That government declined to fund the consumer sector of the economy at a level sufficient to alleviate the double shift for women. Furthermore, the Party, although it endorsed women's rights, endorsed as well a nuclear family which women had to sustain by greater emotional and physical labor than was expected of men. In effect, men retained their dominance in political and economic life, while women increased their participation in the public arena but were still defined very largely by their domestic roles. This was an arrangement that would outlast the Soviet Union itself.

4 / WORLD WAR II
AND ITS AFTERMATH
1941–1953

On June 22, 1941, Adolf Hitler launched the greatest military invasion in history, sending an army of 3.5 million men smashing across the Soviet border. He expected to defeat the Soviet Union in three months; his battle with it lasted nearly four years and ended with him dead, his corpse in the possession of Soviet troops roaming Berlin. But the price the people of the U.S.S.R. paid for this victory was so high that it is difficult to grasp. Perhaps as many as 27 million Soviet citizens died. Seventeen thousand cities and towns and more than 70,000 villages were damaged, and 25 million people were left homeless. The statistics that document the reasons for the Soviet victory are equally staggering: more than 20 million people served in the military, while the civilian population labored in the factories to produce 100,000 tanks, 130,000 aircraft, 800,000 field guns and mortars, and 19 million machine guns, rifles, and pistols.

In every dimension of the Soviet war effort—its heroism, its sacrifice, its profligate expenditure of human life and treasure—women were involved. They were soldiers, workers, and victims. The long-term consequences of the war for women are more difficult to assess. It is clear that the war contributed to the continuation of women's double shift because it confirmed the Party leaders' conviction that heavy industry and the military should be funded at the expense of the consumer sector of the economy. The war's long-term impact on those Soviet values and institutions most important to gender relations seems to have been minimal, perhaps because the war itself lasted only four years.

WOMEN'S PARTICIPATION IN THE WAR

In the Armed Forces

Well over 1 million women served in the Soviet military during World War II. At their peak enlistment in 1943, they were 800,000 to 1,000,000 strong, 8 percent of all troops, regulars and partisans. This was by far the largest recruitment of women undertaken by any of the combatant nations; by contrast, the U.S. Women's Army Corps numbered 100,000 women at its peak in 1945. The precedent for bringing women into the army had been set during the Russian civil war, and the high Soviet death toll made their participation a necessity in World War II.

Overwhelmingly these women were young, unmarried, and ethnically European. Most were volunteers. In the memoirs they wrote later, female veterans said that they had enlisted because they wanted to take part with men in defeating the Germans, because they wanted to avenge killed relatives, or simply because all their friends were going and the battle seemed a great adventure. Some were undoubtedly also pressured into enlisting by the Komsomol, the Party's youth organization. In the first months of the war most female recruits were skilled workers—doctors and nurses, communications experts, truck drivers, engineers, and women who had studied demolitions in the volunteer civil-defense groups organized in the 1930s. As the demand for replacements mounted, younger women just out of high school were given minimal training behind the lines and then rushed to the front.

The Soviet high command did not assign women to a separate women's army corps as did the British and U.S. militaries. Women served in all-female units within the larger command structure or, less commonly, in units that were sexually integrated. Most female soldiers worked in the support services common to all armies—that is, they were nurses, medics and doctors, truck drivers, telephone and telegraph operators, clerks and cooks. Women constituted about 70 percent of the personnel in some communications and transport units. In front-line medical units they were 41 percent of physicians and 43 percent of physicians' assistants. Officially these were all noncombat troops, but they often came under fire, even the medical personnel, for the Germans regularly bombed convoys and hospitals. As had been the case in the Russian civil war, many a nurse, doctor, or engineer carried weapons and used them when necessary.

Women in the Red Army in World War II also served as low-ranking political officers. For example, by 1943 the majority of political officers in the air corps were women. Charged with maintaining the morale of the troops, they held propaganda lectures, published unit newspapers, and ran soldiers' clubs. Those who were assigned to the front often took part in battles. It was a female political officer, Anna Nikulina, who raised the first Soviet flag over the German Chancellery, the headquarters of Hitler's government in Berlin. Nikulina had made the red flag herself, and on the evening of May 2, 1945, she and four soldiers under her command fought their way up to the attic of the Chancellery, climbed through the roof, and proudly unfurled it over the rubble of the Thousand-Year Reich.

Several thousand women (the exact figures are unknown) were sent into combat. In the infantry they served as snipers, machine gunners, sappers, and artillerywomen. In armored divisions they drove tanks, and in the air corps they flew bombers and fighters, as well as worked in ground crews that maintained the aircraft. The government and the military high command had no intention of deploying large numbers of women in combat assignments, but they were willing to make exceptions when they had to. Small training programs for female fighter and bomber crews were set up in 1941 because of the huge losses taken by the Soviet air forces. Women who had come to the front to work in support positions were also sometimes reassigned to combat as the casualties mounted.

Women in combat units suffered along with men from the horrors of war, from exposure to the elements, and from chronic shortages of supplies. Years later Sofia Iurkova, a parachute rigger and antiaircraft gunner, remembered days when she walked for miles, her bedroll on her back and a spoon thrust into her boot, hoping for a meal that never came. Women like Iurkova also learned to cope with primitive equipment. Perhaps the fighting machine most famously associated with Soviet servicewomen was the Po-2 bomber, the workhorse of the all-female 588th Bomber Regiment. It was a wooden biplane used only at night because it was too slow to evade German defenses in daylight. The Po-2 carried a crew of two women, the pilot in the forward cockpit and the navigator-bombardier in the rear. Crew members were armed only with a machine gun, and not always with that. They rode in the open air (for the plane had no canopy) through snowstorms and rain, navigating with the maps they had brought along and with the aid of whatever landmarks they could see below them. The women became skilled at finding their way in the dark, for only on moonless nights could they be reasonably sure that the Germans would not spot them before they were over the targets. In her memoirs, bombardier-navigator Natalia Kravtsova described the Po-2 in terms that would apply to much of the equipment of the Red Army: "We liked our 'night bomber,' even though it was so unsophisticated and unassuming. It was a bold machine and a hard-working one: it worked all night from dusk to dawn without any respite."[1]

All female soldiers, whether combat or support troops, also had to cope with the enormous physical and emotional toll of the war. Death and serious injury were commonplace. Those who survived lived in makeshift housing and went for days or weeks without enough food or sleep, not to mention baths or clean clothes. Available evidence suggests that women bore these burdens as well as men did. For women, however, there was the additional challenge of adjusting to life in the predominantly male world of the military. Most seem to have relied for support on the other members of their unit, just as men did. Women also report in their memoirs that they tried to bring what they saw as feminine touches to the front by cleaning offices and tents and then sprucing them up with flowers, pictures cut from magazines, even embroidered tablecloths. Some women kept dresses in their baggage, and report delight on those few occasions when they could wear them. Women also put their own distinctive decorations on the weapons of war. A member of the 586th Women's Fighter Regiment, Lilia Litvak (whose first name means lily in Russian), flew a Yak fighter with a large lily painted on the fuselage into the air battles over Stalingrad.

---

1 Quoted in K. J. Cottam, *The Golden-Tressed Soldier* (Manhattan, KS, 1983), 9–10.

Men and women also had to adjust to working together. Male soldiers objected to women being at the front on the same grounds as their fathers had done during the civil war. They charged that women could not handle the stresses, that they disrupted the camaraderie of the men, and that they were bad luck. Women in command positions had the additional problem of establishing their authority over resistant subordinates. Undoubtedly some women were subjected to overt sexual abuse. But female veterans wrote in their memoirs that usually they found acceptance once they had proved themselves able to do their jobs. Probably many soldiers were persuaded also by the obvious demand for women's labor. And for some men, women were a pleasant reminder of the peacetime world they were fighting for. On the whole, the female veterans reported that men extended them protection and affection, as well as respect. There were, of course, romances, for the soldiers of both sexes were young and death was very near.

Soviet women also did military service away from the front, as partisans operating behind German lines. Estimates placed the number of female partisans in Belorussia in 1944 at 16 percent of the underground fighters in that region; nationwide they were 10 percent of all partisans. These women were not often commanders but rather soldiers of the underground, performing many of the same jobs as men. They sabotaged communications, sniped at German patrols, and mingled with the civilian population to gather intelligence on troop movements. Some female partisans were double agents, working for the German occupiers. They also nursed wounded comrades and did most of the cooking and cleaning for their units, as well as battled the opposition of some men to their being in the underground. Those who were captured (and they were many) were usually tortured and executed.

Thousands more Soviet women performed military service in civil defense. Working in teams with adolescents and older men, women dug and repaired trenches, maintained barrage balloons, and operated searchlights and antiaircraft batteries. Within cities they removed unexploded bombs and mines, and fought fires.

In the Labor Force

While the contribution of Soviet women to the military in World War II was considerable, the part they played in the civilian labor force, both industrial and agricultural, was extraordinary. Of course women joined the paid labor force in all the combatant nations, as they had done in World War I. But nowhere did they make so major a contribution to victory as in the Soviet Union, for there the majority of civilian workers was female. Women had constituted 38 percent of the nonagricultural labor force in 1940; by 1943 that figure had climbed to 57 percent. (By comparison, women constituted 37 percent of the paid labor force in the United States in 1945.) Female participation in certain geographic regions and economic sectors was even greater. Close to the front, women usually made up the great majority of civilian workers. Occupations and manufacturing sectors with a predominantly female workforce before the war became even more so: by 1945, 80 to 90 percent of the workers in light industry were women. Women were 52 percent of all collective farmers in 1941, 80 percent in 1945. Even in economic sectors where men had previously been in the great majority, the ranks of women grew. By 1944, 41 percent of the coal miners in the mining centers of the Donets Basin of southern Ukraine were female.

Female workers moved not only from one type of employment to another. They moved geographically, fleeing the front in the first years of the war for towns in the rear to which manufacturing was relocated, and then returning to the liberated west as the Red Army drove the Germans out. Women moved upward in the labor force as well, into more skilled manual labor and into managerial positions vacated by men. This was especially true on the collective farms, where women in large numbers now became tractor drivers, mechanics, accountants, and brigade leaders.

Promotions into positions once held by men brought higher wages, but no raise in pay could compensate for the enormous hardships of daily life during the war years. Many women suffered financially during the war because they lost the support of their husbands' income when the men were drafted. Military allotments were far lower than most men's peacetime pay and were often late in coming because of government inefficiency. The government also cruelly removed from the rolls of military dependents the wives of the millions of Soviet POWs held by the Germans, on the grounds that these men had betrayed their country by being captured.

All women had to cope with worsening working conditions. Insistent upon maximizing production, the government suspended the always lax enforcement of health and safety regulations, and it increased penalties for absenteeism. Women now worked ten- to twelve-hour days for weeks on end. Peasant women endured even more gruelling conditions because so many men from the countryside were taken away to the army, as were the trucks, horses, and oxen that usually helped with the work. Then a growing shortage of spare parts made it difficult to repair even that equipment which was left, so that throughout the war, women, old men, and children had to do most of the work of farming by hand.

The women of the Soviet labor force also coped with extraordinarily difficult living conditions. Life was easier the farther one got from the battlefront, so that women in Central Asia and Siberia, particularly the largely self-sufficient peasants and hunter-gatherers, suffered less than those who lived to the west. But the great majority of women actually lived in the west. With virtually no consumer goods available, they had to mend again oft-mended clothes, get by with less soap, and barter with their neighbors for necessities. These were skills that Soviet women, long accustomed to poverty, had already mastered. More difficult to overcome were the persistent shortages of food.

Because the war was fought on much of the best Soviet farmland, because so many peasants were drafted and so many farm machines sat idle for lack of spare parts, and because government procurements focused on feeding the troops, the food supplies in the villages dwindled. Throughout the nation, food was rationed to everyone except collective farmers (who received none on the grounds that they could provide for themselves). The rationing system favored the elite, the military, and skilled workers, but even those groups did not fare very well. Most Soviet women subsisted throughout the war on bread and potatoes.

EKATERINA MIKHAILOVA

Ekaterina Mikhailova was one of the 100,000 Soviet women decorated for their military service in World War II. Born in 1925, the daughter of working-class Leningraders, Mikhailova grew up an orphan, cared for by her brother and sister. In June 1941 she was a sixteen-year-old nursing student on her way to visit her brother when Germany attacked the Soviet Union. Mikhailova immediately signed up for the army and soon was fighting with partisan units outside Moscow; there in the fall of 1941 she was seriously wounded.

Mikhailova had always loved the sea, so when she recovered from her injuries she requested a transfer to the navy. For the next year she worked as a nurse aboard medical ships transporting the wounded down the Volga. This assignment bored her, however, and in 1943 she volunteered for the marines. Three times local commanders refused her because she was a very small woman, who, they believed, would not be able to cope with the rigors of front-line duty. Mikhailova appealed to higher authorities and finally received the assignment she wanted, as a combat nurse with the marines of the Azov fleet. From the summer of 1943 on through 1944, she fought with these troops across the Crimea, along the coast of the Black Sea, and up the Danube River. Mikhailova became a valued member of her unit, earning the respect of the once dubious men by sharing their hardships and taking care of them. Routinely she braved enemy fire, machine gun in one hand, medic's bag in the other, to tend to wounded comrades. The men made up affectionate songs about the fortitude of "Our Katusha," her nickname, which was also the name of the famous, deadly, Soviet rocket launcher.

Mikhailova's most famous exploit came in December 1944, during the assault on Ilok, a Yugoslav river town. She was assigned to a small diversionary unit that was to land at night on an island below the town and draw the attention of the German defenders away from the main Soviet force. The fifty marines came up on the island in the dark, only to find it covered with several feet of icy-cold water. They took refuge in the trees and opened fire as ordered. For the next two hours, despite a wounded hand, Mikhailova waded from tree to tree, tying the wounded down so that they would not fall into the flooding river and then treating them as best she could. When reinforcements arrived, she was ferried almost unconscious to a hospital ship. The fleet commanders recommended Mikhailova for the nation's highest military award, Hero of the Soviet Union, but authorities in Moscow refused to approve the nomination because they thought the reports of her valor exaggerated. Instead she received the less prestigious Order of the Red Banner. By then Mikhailova had run away from the hospital where she was recuperating, to rejoin her unit. She stayed with it to Vienna.

When the war ended, Mikhailova returned to Leningrad. Her brother and sister had both died in the war, so she lived alone and worked her way through medical school. After graduating she settled down in the nearby town of Elektrostal, married an engineer, had a son, and made a career as a physician in a neighborhood clinic. She kept the stories of her military service to herself until the early 1960s, when Soviet journalists tracked her down to make a television documentary about her. Mikhailova spent her later years as a respected member of her community, strolling through city parks on holidays in a marine tunic decked with medals.

City dwellers attempted to supplement these staples by growing their own food in vacant lots and trading with people from the countryside. But the general picture was of pervasive malnutrition among people in countryside and city, and increases in the rates of epidemic disease. That women could stay at their jobs and work as exhaustingly as they did is all the more remarkable when set against this background of terrible hardship and need.

WOMEN IN THE ICONOGRAPHY OF THE WAR

Women also played a central role in the wartime mobilization of national patriotism, for Soviet propagandists publicized the deeds of real heroines as well as exploiting popular notions about women to rally support for the war effort. Perhaps the most famous of the real Soviet heroines of World War II was Zoia Kosmodemianskaia, known also by her underground alias, "Tanya." Tanya was a nineteen-year-old partisan captured by the Germans in December 1941. After withstanding brutal torture without betraying her comrades, she bravely went to her public execution, calling on the assembled peasants to fight for the motherland. Her story was much publicized both during and after the war, and she became a symbol of dedication and selflessness to several generations of Soviet youth.

Another famous heroine of World War II was Maria Oktiabrskaia. She and her husband were both Party members; they had taken the name October to show their dedication to communism. (The word referred to the October Revolution that had brought the Bolsheviks to power.) Oktiabrskaia decided to go to the front when her husband, her two sons, and her parents were killed in the war. Hating the German invaders and determined to take them on personally, she raised 50,000 rubles, then arranged to donate the money to finance construction of a tank on condition that she be permitted to command it. The Red Army authorities agreed, and Oktiabrskaia christened her T-34 "Fighting Comrade-in-Arms." She and her crew, her "sons" as she called them, made themselves famous in battles across Belorussia. Valiant to the point of foolhardiness, Oktiabrskaia was killed in the winter of 1944 as she knelt down to repair the track of her tank in the middle of a battle.

Many women in the Red Army performed as heroically as Tanya and Oktiabrskaia; by the end of the war more than 100,000 women had received military decorations. Propagandists picked up their stories and publicized them, stressing the women's courage and endurance. In addition to emphasizing these martial virtues usually regarded as masculine, the journalists also idealized the care women lavished on their male comrades, whom they nursed and looked after. This was not an inaccurate portrayal, but the prominence given to women's nurturing men suggests also that the propagandists felt it necessary to reassure their audience that the heroines of the Red Army had preserved both their femininity and their appropriate relationship to men despite the brutalizing conditions of war.

Soviet propagandists presented the extraordinary exploits of real women such as Tanya and Oktiabrskaia to a public hungry for heroines. They also drew on idealized images of woman in their efforts to rally Soviet morale. In particular, they made a point of calling on everyone to fight for "the motherland," resurrecting an ancient Russian word, *rodina*, that communist propaganda had earlier scorned as a relic of traditional society. Now anxious to arouse any loyalties to the group, even traditional ones, propagandists teamed this feminine *rodina* with a masculine, fatherly symbol, the image of Stalin, and exhorted Soviet troops to rush into battle shouting, "For the Motherland! For Stalin!" Millions did.

"Motherland" was a symbol that had a multiplicity of associations for Russians and all the other nationalities fighting in the Red Army. The etymological root of *rodina* lay in Russian words for "kinfolk" and "ancestors"; in modern usage the word referred to the Russian land itself, the mother earth, as well as to one's home village or town. In defending the *rodina*, soldiers were thus fighting both for the land and for female kin—mothers, wives, and sweethearts—who remained behind on that land. This was not just the poetical conceit of the propagandists; the Germans were in fact destroying both the Soviet countryside and the women who lived there. But *rodina* also evoked fond memories of a timeless ancestral world for which the army fought, a world without war, a world of natural beauty, family love, and domestic comforts.

In the propaganda of all the combatant nations of World War II, women were associated with nature, the family, and home. But propagandists differed from country to country in which aspects of the idealized female they emphasized. In the United States, the women featured in propaganda posters and films were likely to be young, stylishly dressed, and sexy. British posters often portrayed beautiful young mothers holding smiling babies. By contrast, the woman favored by Soviet propagandists was a middle-aged mother. To evoke hatred of the invaders she was often portrayed as victimized by the war, fleeing from the Germans, or mourning the loss of her children. To stir up feelings of resistance, she was shown in attitudes of defiance, standing firmly on her native soil and admonishing her children to fight. The Soviet equivalent of the American recruiting poster "Uncle Sam Wants You" featured not a male commander stabbing his finger at the viewer, but a middle-aged peasant woman who beckons the viewer to follow her. Over her is emblazoned the message "The Motherland Is Calling." She is typical of the iconography of Soviet propaganda. She is European, not Asian. She is dressed for work. Far from vulnerable, like the delicate madonnas of the British posters for example, this woman is a stocky, strong, maternal authority figure who calls the young to war. Idealized though she was, she did fairly represent one of the essential virtues of millions of Soviet women—their hardy endurance.

THE EFFECTS OF THE WAR ON THE FAMILY

Naturally people tried to survive the war by holding on to family ties. The marriage rate shot up in the summer of 1941, just as the Germans came plunging through the country's defenses; people rushed to marry before the draft carried men away. Marriage could not keep them at home, however, and millions of women spent the war on their own. Near the front and far behind the lines, they struggled to feed their children and to maintain their contacts with relatives and friends. Many found that nothing they could do prevailed against the ferocious tide of destruction. Death and long separations from family members became normal. As in World War I, millions of children were orphaned. After the summer of 1941 the marriage rate fell off precipitously and remained low until late 1944. The birth rate fell as well, of course; demographers estimate that only half as many children were born during the war as would have been born had it not occurred. There is no evidence, however, that the multitude of personal tragedies brought any lasting change in prevailing Soviet notions about family life.

The authorities were seriously worried, as they had been during the NEP years, that the upheaval would have long-term effects on family stability. Thus they took steps in 1944 to encourage monogamy and a high birthrate. A new marriage law raised the legal fees charged for divorce to a point where few people could afford it, and also attempted to encourage marriage by denying illegitimate children the right to support by their fathers. The effect of this measure was softened somewhat by another decree that guaranteed government-financed child-support benefits to single mothers.

It was also in 1944 that the Soviet government launched the much-publicized "mother-heroine" campaigns. Women who bore more than two children received cash bonuses on the birth of each additional child, the award rising to the substantial sum of 5,000 rubles when the tenth baby arrived. Women with seven or more children also received medals and were written up in the Soviet press. The heroine-mother awards continued on after the war, becoming the source of many Soviet jokes, but having little impact on the birthrate. The birth and marriage rates did begin to rise late in 1944, but this was more a response to improving economic conditions and the approaching end to the war than to governmental stimuli.

THE AFTERMATH OF WAR, 1945-1953

When the war ended and indeed for decades afterwards, Soviet people, women as well as men, drew a tremendous sense of achievement from their victory. World War I had destroyed the tsarist government and brought the country to civil war. This time the communist government, despite its many shortcomings, had risen to the enormous challenge of managing both the military and the economy, and the people had rallied to triumph over a monstrous enemy. In doing so, the one-time pariah state, earlier shunned and feared by the "respectable" capitalist democracies of the West, had earned a new standing among the great powers.

The joy of victory resolved itself into long-lasting pride. But the Soviet people could not celebrate the end of the war with the sort of unrestrained jubilation that filled the streets of New York in 1945. There were so many dead to mourn, so many wounded to care for, and so much to rebuild. Margaret Wettlin, an American teacher who lived in the Soviet Union, movingly described a church service in Moscow in June 1945, in which she and the congregation tried to come to grips with the nation's death toll:

> "Our Father," prayed the priest, "Our only source of solace. . . ." A groan rose from the congregation, and it was like a choral response in Greek tragedy. Twenty million. Here was the humanity behind the statistics. I looked at the faces around me. Mostly they were the faces of elderly women framed in kerchiefs, seamed and hardened by too much experience of life. But there were also many younger women with children. It was a congregation of wives and mothers desperately seeking support in their hour of need.
>
> Somebody tapped me on the shoulder and handed me a note, indicating that I was to pass it up to the altar. Then I noticed that everybody was passing up these notes. Each note named someone for whom a prayer was to be offered for the repose of his soul.[2]

Such women went to work, clearing streets of debris, burying the dead, planting the fields, finding homes for orphans, and getting children back to school. Reconstruction lasted throughout the decade and into the 1950s. Official Soviet estimates calculated that the war had cost 1,890 billion rubles, a sum equivalent to the total prewar income of the Soviet people for seven years. One third of that total came from the loss of

---

2 Margaret Wettlin, *Fifty Russian Winters: An American Woman's Life in the Soviet Union* (New York, 1992), 254.

property. Six million buildings had been destroyed, as well as 65,000 kilometers of railroad track, 40,000 schools, 43,000 public libraries. All this, and the coal mines, power stations, telephone exchanges, and everything else had to be rebuilt. Naturally severe austerity continued. There was famine in Ukraine, and hunger elsewhere in the late 1940s. But by the time Stalin died in March 1953 the economic infrastructure had been restored.

Social reconstruction also proceeded successfully, indeed rapidly. Families reassembled what was left of their kin, people married, children were born. So many young men had died that millions of young women never found husbands. But this did not affect the postwar reassertion of the values that had prevailed before the war in city and countryside, except perhaps to make people more convinced than ever of the importance of marriage and family.

The process of restoration had a short-lived, negative aspect; people shunned the women who had served in the military. Some said that the female veterans had been hardened by their experience and were no longer feminine. Others charged that those at the front had been sexually promiscuous. "Who have you got married to?" wailed Tamara Umniagina's new mother-in-law to her soldier-son in 1945. "An army girl. Why, you have two younger sisters. Who will marry them now?"[3]

Perhaps some of this cruelty expressed the guilt of those who had not fought, but more probably it was simply part of the restoration of social order. Distinctions between masculine and feminine, blurred by the war, were being redrawn. History's periodic redefinitions of gender, often conservative in tendency, have not usually been kind to liberated women, and these recent war heroines were no exception. Stinging from the injustice of it all, female veterans learned to hide the fact that they had served.

The war had little long-term effect on women's position in the labor force. Soviet women were not laid off in large numbers after the war, as were U.S. women. The crucial role women's labor had played in winning the war, and the colossal task of rebuilding that lay ahead, only strengthened the government's

3 S. S. Alexiyevich, *War's Unwomanly Face* (Moscow, 1985), 244.

commitment to their working. Men did move back into those specialties where they had predominated before the war, displacing some women. This was particularly true in agriculture, where men reclaimed the leadership positions on the collective farms, but it occurred in heavy industry as well. For years after the war, women's advancement in the paid labor force may also have been affected by the policy of giving male veterans preferential treatment in education, employment, and recruitment into the Party. Women kept some of the gains in employment that they had made, however; for example, it was during World War II that they reached a statistical crossover point and actually became the majority of Soviet physicians, a situation that has not altered since.

As the economy was rebuilt and everyday life was restored to its prewar patterns, the government returned as well to its old habits of control and persecution. The Stalin dictatorship had eased during the war years, both because the regime could not wield its power effectively in the turmoil and also because it wanted to cultivate public support. But the great victory emboldened Stalin, who had, in any case, never been timid about asserting himself. After the war he pushed the Soviet Union into an unprecedented prominence in world affairs, seizing control of the new governments of Eastern Europe and challenging the United States for influence in central Europe. He also instructed his ministers, particularly those at the NKVD, to restore central control over Soviet society.

Mass arrests began again almost before the war ended. POWs returned from Germany were accused of having collaborated with the enemy by allowing themselves to be captured and were shipped off to the GULAG. Several nationality groups—the Germans who had lived along the southern shores of the Volga River for 150 years, the Crimean Tatars, the Ossetians of the Caucasus—were accused of having collaborated and were deported to Siberia. Later in the 1940s, intellectuals, particularly Jewish ones, were accused of political conspiracies or anti-Soviet ideas and were sent to prison. This reapplication of the Terror was accompanied by a barrage of propaganda that emphasized the superiority of communism to capitalism. Banished were the appeals to religion that had flourished during the war. The climate of fear that this persecution created made the late 1940s a time of high anxiety and deep disappointment in the Soviet Union. Many had hoped that the spirit of the war— the spirit of people pulling together and trusting one another— would survive to lighten the burdens of reconstruction.

CONCLUSIONS

Soviet women played a central role in the defeat of Nazi Germany because they were able to take men's places and make the weapons and grow the food that made the victory possible. Their ability to cope with hardship had never been more essential to the survival of their people. Yet the war, for all its power to destroy individual lives, appears not to have significantly altered those Soviet institutional arrangements and values that affected women most directly. The massive disruption, far from provoking change as the revolution had done, inspired instead a strong desire for stability, for a return to prewar arrangements. This conservatism found expression after the war in a reassertion of domestic values and associated ideas about women. It also found expression in the leaders' brutality. Only after Stalin died did Soviet women enter a new era, one marked not by terror or social upheaval but rather by prolonged peace and eased domestic pressures.

5 / PEACETIME
1953–1982

Joseph Stalin died on March 5, 1953. He left the Soviet Union a great power, the supreme exemplar of an ideology and a productive system that were copied by governments around the world. He also left the nation traumatized and severely damaged by his arbitrary regime. His successors tried to remedy the worst Stalinist abuses, first by reining in the police and freeing most political prisoners from the GULAG, then by improving living and working conditions. The path they took to reform was somewhat circuitous and often rather bumpy, but they pursued it doggedly. Their record was generally one of success until the late 1970s. The economy recovered from the war and then grew steadily, the standard of living rose, and the Soviet Union enjoyed the longest period of domestic tranquility in its history. Internationally it was one of the two great Superpowers, admired and imitated by, and exerting tremendous influence over, many peoples around the world. Its satellites and cosmonauts were circling the globe by the early 1960s, while its athletes, musicians, and dancers were winning awards everywhere they performed.

Women all over the vast country benefitted from the Soviet Union's successes. They enjoyed expanded opportunities for education and employment and lived far easier lives than their mothers and grandmothers had known. They took pride in their country's accomplishments, to which they had made such an important contribution. They also expected their prospects to continue to improve. Economic growth did not end the double shift, however, for the government continued to favor heavy industry over the consumer sector of the economy. Nor was there any fundamental reconsideration of the New Soviet Woman. Rather the improvements in women's lives throughout the Soviet

Union after World War II were contained within the patterns and practices established in the twenties and thirties.

URBAN WOMEN'S LIVES IN THE POSTWAR YEARS

By the 1960s the typical Soviet woman lived in a city and worked in an office. She was a high-school graduate. She married when she was in her early twenties, soon had one child, saved her money, and after several years of living with her parents or her in-laws, moved with her husband and child into a two-room apartment of their own in one of the massive new buildings in the suburbs. They scrimped and saved for new clothes, furniture, a television, and vacations on the Black Sea. She had few luxuries by Western European standards, or even by her own, but her life was probably easier than her mother's had been.

Education and Participation in the Paid Labor Force

Perhaps the most important improvement for such women in the postwar years came in education. Of course there were significant differences from region to region in the Soviet Union and between the various nationality groups, but by the 1970s the majority of Soviet women had at least a high-school education, and females made up half of all students studying at universities and in postsecondary vocational programs. This was a substantial improvement in a society where only two generations before most women had been unable even to sign their names.

Women also moved ahead in the work world. Most important, the majority no longer did heavy manual labor in the cities but instead held service, clerical, administrative, and professional jobs. More women managed factories and occupied administrative positions in central government ministries in the Soviet Union than was the case in many Western European nations in the 1950s and 1960s. There were also many more women in the professions in the Soviet Union than elsewhere, particularly in fields such as engineering or medicine that were dominated by men in the West. In 1974 for example, 70 percent of Soviet physicians were women, as compared to 7 percent in the United States. Thousands of Soviet women worked as architects, lawyers, judges, scientists, and university professors. There were also many women prominent in sports (Soviet female athletes regularly took home medals from international competitions), in the arts (the ballerinas of the Kirov and Bolshoi companies achieved international fame), and in the literary world (where a new generation of writers and poets came of age). These and all the millions of less accomplished women who made the transition from field or factory to office raised their income and bettered their working conditions.

Yet the similarities between women's situation in the labor force in the U.S.S.R. and Western Europe were also striking. Despite the fact that a far higher percentage of Soviet women worked outside the home, very few had made it into the upper echelons of the nation's economic or political leadership. Rather, the great majority occupied the lower ranks of white-collar occupations and professions. For example, most Soviet physicians were women, but the most prestigious jobs in medicine— teaching and research in the major hospitals in the large cities— overwhelmingly were held by men. Female doctors worked long hours in neighborhood clinics dispensing primary care, for which they were paid less than skilled blue-collar workers. An analogous situation prevailed in engineering, where men ran the projects and women made the blueprints. Female workers were also still clustered in certain sectors of the economy—food supply, textile and clothing manufacture, the arts, education, and medicine—that were poorly funded and therefore poorly paid. As a consequence, in the 1960s and 1970s, Soviet women earned 60 to 70 percent of what men earned, a differential little changed since the 1920s. Approximately the same difference between women's and men's wages prevailed throughout the European world.

Most important of all, women were only minor players in the most powerful organization in the U.S.S.R., the Communist Party. Female Party membership rose to 26.5 percent (4.5 million women) in 1981. This increase in numbers did not move women up the hierarchy into the regional and national leadership of the Party, however. Rather, most female communists worked in local committees where they specialized in cultural activities and propaganda, assignments that conferred little power. Two to 4 percent of the members of the Central Committee were female, but even they had no power in their own right, having been appointed by powerful men simply to demonstrate the Party's goodwill. The Politburo, the center of power in the Soviet Union, remained an all-male club, despite token appointments made by Khrushchev and Gorbachev. This is not to say that the women who reached the upper ranks of the Party enjoyed no privileges. They held important, well-paid jobs, usually in education, the arts, or the consumer sector of the economy, and they shared with the women married to powerful men the elite's special access to foreign goods, the best medical care, and well-stocked shops. But they remained at a distance from the politics of the all-male inner circles.

The Soviet government did not openly endorse this state of affairs, but it promoted it in a variety of ways. Party leaders had no interest in sharing power with women, and so made only the most minimal, perhaps even deliberately inadequate efforts to advance women's status in the Party. They were somewhat more concerned to improve female participation in the labor force, but here they promulgated policies that were actually counterproductive. The schools taught gender stereotypes and "tracked" girls and boys into different subjects, encouraging boys to study mathematics and girls literature. The government also enforced protective labor regulations that prohibited women from working with molten metals, dangerous chemicals, and heavy weights, as well as from holding jobs classified as particularly dangerous (for instance, aircraft testing and fire fighting). It was true that such work posed special health risks, but it also paid well.

Yet it would be a mistake to minimize the gains that had been made. Despite continuing inequalities, many urban women felt that they had made progress in the postwar years. Spiritually they shared in both the communist idealism and self-congratulatory patriotism of the time, and thrilled, as their husbands and children did, to their nation's exploits in space, athletics, and foreign affairs. They readily agreed that white-collar work, even the most menial, was a real improvement over the dirty, exhausting manual labor that had been the lot of most women in the past. They still complained about working conditions and the other difficulties of their lives, but they also declared, to pollsters and in letters to the press, that they experienced much personal satisfaction from their jobs. They built strong bonds with their coworkers, with whom they shared not only office tasks, but also the chores of shopping. And many Soviet women also accepted the oft-reiterated principle that women should work outside the home in order to be healthy and independent. "I think it's essential for a woman to work," said Natasha, a twenty-two-year-old Muscovite interviewed in the late 1970s. "If I don't work for a period of time, I lose my feeling of self-esteem."[1] This attitude among young women would have delighted Artiukhina, Kollontai, and the other crusaders of the Zhenotdel.

Daily Life in the Cities

Soviet cities prospered in the 1950s and 1960s. Modern apartment blocks rose in the suburbs, while trams, buses, and taxis crowded the streets. Some richer people even owned their own boxy little Lada automobiles. Stores that had remained damaged and empty in the austerity of the late forties were refurbished and stocked with food, domestic appliances, and clothes. By the 1970s there was also a flourishing black market in Western goods, particularly the products of the youth culture—jeans, cosmetics, and recordings of rock music. The social services on which women depended saw a marked expansion. In 1970, 50 percent of urban children were enrolled in day care, and the numbers continued to climb thereafter. The medical system improved facilities for gynecological and maternity care, and maternity leave and benefits for new mothers were increased.

At the same time, the developments in family life that had barely begun in the cities before the turn of the century became prevalent in the lives of Soviet citizens across the U.S.S.R. By the 1960s, the majority of city dwellers of European ethnicity lived in nuclear families, young people chose their mates with a minimum of parental interference, and the birthrate, low since the twenties, remained very low. The numbers of unmarried women among the European nationalities climbed as well, due partly to the shortage of eligible males after the war and the Stalinist terror and partly also to the high divorce rates. By the

---

1 Carola Hansson and Karin Liden, *Moscow Women* (New York, 1983), 165.

mid-1970s almost half of all marriages were ending in divorce. Furthermore, women were living longer than men. The life expectancy of Soviet men actually began to fall in the 1960s, probably largely as a consequence of the fact that men were drinking and smoking more than in the past. That people could now manage to buy vodka and cigarettes regularly was an indication of the country's material gains; that many people abused drugs indicated a spreading spiritual emptiness, ennui, and frustration as the economy faltered in the seventies and the aging leadership proved unable to respond effectively to society's problems.

Toward the end of the 1960s, the postwar economic growth began to slow. Unfortunately for the government, the Soviet people's expectations continued to rise, and by the late 1970s they were becoming increasingly dissatisfied with their lives. They knew that Western Europe's economy was still surging forward, spewing out healthy food and high-quality consumer goods, for they could see these things in glossy magazines and color movies from the West, and they could even buy some of them on the booming Soviet black market. People in the West also appeared to work less and to have more fun. They had long luxurious vacations, nice restaurants, discos and nightclubs, lots of movies, even more interesting television. Or at least so it seemed to Soviet women in Moscow or Kiev or Tallinn, who took what they knew about the West from movies, television, and magazines. By the end of the seventies, they knew that, compared to France or West Germany, their nation remained a poor country with an inefficient economy, governed by leaders who chose to spend a huge percentage of the gross national product on a glittering defense establishment. The housing boom had supplied only small, inadequate apartments, and not enough of them to satisfy demand. The trams were always crowded and the phones often squawked with ear-splitting static. Young people complained that there was nothing interesting to do after school. Even Soviet toys and vacation hotels were shabby and shoddy. And everything was becoming begrimed with the fallout from dangerously rising air pollution.

Indeed, everyday life in the postwar cities, although much easier than it had been several decades earlier, remained difficult. Women, working the double shift, bore the burdens of its manifold problems. Soviet studies showed that they devoted thirty to forty hours a week to housework, the same amount they had spent in the 1920s. Nor had husbands' share of the work increased; as in the past, they spent half as much time on domestic chores as did their wives. Women cooked, they washed and dried clothes in their sinks and bathtubs, they scrubbed the floors and beat the carpets, they fed and clothed their husbands and children. But most of all, they shopped endlessly.

Shopping had long been women's work in Soviet cities. It was so time-consuming not just because goods and food were in perennially short supply, but also because the organization of buying and selling itself was so cumbersome. A woman could not stop off at the supermarket after work to pick up what she needed for dinner, but instead had to go to specialty stores—groceries, butcher shops, bakeries, dairies. It was the same when she shopped for clothes or other consumer goods. At each store she was required to pick out what she wanted, get a hand-written note of the price from the salesclerk, carry that to a cashier, pay the cashier, get a receipt from the cashier, and then take the receipt back to the salesclerk, who would give her whatever she had bought on receipt of this receipt. At each stage of this old-fashioned ritual, which had originated in Russia before the revolution, she would have to stand in line. If she found that the store where she usually shopped had sold out of what she wanted, she would have to walk on to another. And she would have to carry all she had bought from store to store, and through the crowds on trams and busses, and up the long, concrete sidewalks to her apartment building, and then up the stairs.

Soviet women did not accept their situation happily. Like their grandmothers in 1917, they let their anger show on the streets. They grumbled to one another while standing in line and yelled at surly clerks. They pushed and shoved to get into stores. To friends and family they complained about the shortages, the lines, and the crowds; they complained about always being tired; and they complained about their husbands. Lida, a thirty-one-year-old chambermaid from Moscow and a single mother interviewed in the late 1970s, was typical. "At home a woman usually does everything. When the husband comes home he reads his paper and watches T.V., contrary to what the newspapers say. They show men on March 8 [Woman's Day] cooking and cleaning and shopping and scrubbing floors. But it's really the women who do everything."[2]

Women chose to minimize their load by having very few children; one per couple became the norm in the cities. To limit their childbearing they had to resort to numerous abortions. The government did not fund the production of effective contraceptives, because it wanted to increase the birthrate and because in general its attention to personal health services was often negligent. So most urban women in the postwar years had many abortions, six or seven being not uncommon. All this—the strain of the double shift and poor medical care—took a toll on women's health, leading to rising rates of infant and maternal mortality in the 1960s and 1970s. By the end of the 1970s, many women in Soviet cities were feeling overworked and out of patience. It did not mollify them when government propaganda pointed out, with justifiable pride, how much better off they were than their grandmothers had been, for they were no longer content to measure their situation by such a miserable standard.

RURAL WOMEN'S LIVES—THE EUROPEAN POPULATION

Throughout the postwar decades, life was harder in the countryside than in the cities, and patriarchal traditions remained relatively strong there. By the middle sixties women in the villages of Ukraine, Siberia, and central Russia still followed the rhythms of nature's year, rising before dawn to tend the cows through the long winter, shepherding the ewes with their lambs through the hesitant, untrustworthy spring. They still spent the summers in the fields and forests, planting and harvesting. The work was in many ways just as gruelling as it had ever been, for women mostly worked with their hands and hoes while men drove the machinery and managed the farms. But change, on the other hand, continued. The great gulf between city and village nar-

2 Ibid., 110.

rowed considerably after 1953, as education improved and electronic communications brought the city closer than ever before. Women could now look beyond the edge of the fields that surrounded their villages, they could travel to the larger world or bring it into their simple wooden houses by turning on the radio or television. The result was a quiet but very real change in women's attitudes, amounting almost to a rural revolution.

Education and Participation in the Paid Labor Force

Rural women, as well as urban ones, made impressive strides in education in the postwar era, overcoming a centuries-old disparity between themselves and men. In 1959, 30 percent of men but only 23 percent of women living in the countryside across the Soviet Union had attended secondary school. By 1979, 44 percent of all rural women, and well over 90 percent of those younger than 30, had gone to high school. Sixteen percent had studied at an institution of higher education. Overall, women outpaced men in formal schooling, so that by 1980 many wives in the countryside in the European U.S.S.R. were better educated than their husbands.

But peasants were even less able than urban women to translate their greater education into career advancement. For a hundred years, women in the countryside had been excluded from the best blue-collar jobs; this did not change after 1953. In fact, the percentages of women operating farm machinery actually fell in the postwar period, despite government campaigns in the 1970s to recruit female tractor drivers. Women were also less well represented in the professions in the countryside than in the cities, though there were indeed more female biologists, agronomists, teachers, doctors, and journalists in rural areas than there had ever been before. Women still could not break through to the ranks of managers on collective or state farms; in fact the percentage of women in leadership positions actually declined. In 1943, a peak year, women occupied 12 percent of managerial posts on the farms (a small enough percentage, given the crisis of the war); by 1960 that figure had fallen to 6 percent, where it remained for the rest of the Soviet period. Nikita Khrushchev, the often outspoken First Secretary of the Party, summed up the situation when he harangued an agricultural conference in Kiev in 1961, "You are well aware of the enormous role which women play in all aspects of building communism. But for some reason there are few women in this hall. You have to use a pair of binoculars to spot them. How do you explain this? You can say that it's mainly managers who are here. It turns out that it's the men who do the managing and the women who do the work."[3]

So it was understandable that young women from the European areas of the country began moving to the cities in droves. The simple fact is that they were fed up with the hard work and social conservatism of the countryside. According to the 1970 census, the rural population aged fifteen to thirty in the Russian republic was 52 percent male and 48 percent female, despite the fact that women made up 54 percent of the republic's total population. Furthermore, those leaving were the better-educated young women. They went with their parents' blessings. Mothers interviewed by Soviet researchers declared that they wanted their girls to find jobs in the cities so that they would not grow old and haggard before their time. "Her father and I have spent our whole lives in muck and filth," declared one such mother. "Let Zina do other work."[4]

Daily Life in the Countryside

Young women also went to the cities to escape village living conditions. Although there was improvement in rural housing and transportation in the postwar years, and in electricity and natural gas supplied to the villages, most country folk continued to live without indoor plumbing or central heating. Their stores were poorly stocked and they endured worse medical care than city people. Rural schools were short of books and maps while day care in the 1970s was available to only 12 percent of rural children. Farming families knew that life was better in the cities, for not only had many of them travelled there, but most of them could see every night on television the way city people lived.

---

3 *Izvestiia*, 26 December 1961.
4 *Molodoi kommunist*, 9 (1977): 86, quoted in Susan Bridger, *Women in the Soviet Countryside* (Cambridge, 1987), 211.

ANNA
AKHMATOVA

direct, honest, and passionate, delicately crafted and very beautiful. Later Akhmatova broadened her subject matter to consider the tragedies of Russia's twentieth-century history and deepened her powers of expression. Her *Requiem* and *Poem Without a Hero* rank among the most moving creations of twentieth-century poetry.

Akhmatova developed her talents despite almost continuous persecution from the Soviet authorities. In the 1920s she was widely condemned in the press as a "bourgeois" writer interested in the insignificant, even indecent subjects of religion and romantic love. Unable thereafter to publish her poems but determined not to emigrate, Akhmatova supported herself by doing translations. Her outward submission did not mollify the Stalinist leadership. In 1937 her son, Lev Gumilev, was arrested. To express her anguish, however privately, she wrote a collection of poems on the purges, *Requiem*, that recorded the suffering of those

Anna Akhmatova (1889–1966) was a supremely accomplished Russian poet. The daughter of a maritime engineer and a Russian noblewoman, Akhmatova was educated in St. Petersburg. She began publishing her lyrical explorations of the pain of lost love in the years just before the revolution. These early poems were condemned to wait for their imprisoned loved ones. Gumilev was released fairly soon and during World War II Akhmatova even returned to official favor. But in August 1946, Andrei Zhdanov, the Politburo member who led the postwar repression of the intelligentsia, singled her out for another attack. Again her son was arrested.

The persecution of both Akhmatova and Gumilev ended only after Stalin's death. In the late 1950s Akhmatova was permitted to publish again, although *Requiem* and *Poem Without a Hero* remained unacceptable to the censors. By the early 1960s, her work had been widely translated and was receiving international acclaim. Her admirers saw Akhmatova as an exemplar of all that was finest in the Russian intelligentsia, its integrity, artistry, and endurance. This newfound fame pleased her but also made her uneasy, so accustomed to anonymity had she grown. Her final victory came twenty years after her death, when, in the late 1980s, her complete works were published in her homeland.

Urban values, borne on electronic airwaves in the postwar years, continued to penetrate the villages, narrowing the chasm that had once divided country from city. Soviet public opinion surveys rather surprisingly revealed in the 1960s that the majority of rural people now embraced the values of the modern nuclear family; that is, they believed that marriages should be based primarily on love and companionship, not economic considerations. Parents were exercising much less influence over their children's choice of marriage partners. Young couples set up their own households as soon as they could afford it and reared far fewer children than did earlier generations. The rural birthrate fell even faster than the urban, so that by the 1970s there was very little difference in family size between urban and rural people of European nationality.

And finally, patriarchalism's influence on the behavior of wives and husbands was diminishing. Rural women of the European nationalities reported to pollsters in the 1960s and 1970s that they enjoyed a greater voice in family decision-making and were respected more by their husbands than previously, an improvement they attributed to their being better educated. Another sign of their growing confidence and independence was the fact that they were also far more willing to leave marriages that failed than they had ever been. The rural divorce rate doubled among the European nationalities in the 1970s, and the majority of those suing for divorce were women. It was still difficult to be a single person in a small village, and consequently even after the sharp increase in rural divorce rates, only one-quarter of marriages in the countryside ended in divorce, as compared to one-half of urban ones. This represented a significant change, however, for it indicated that thousands of women were now walking out on the alcoholism and routine abuse their grandmothers had simply endured.

WOMEN'S LIVES—THE NON-EUROPEAN POPULATION

The ways of the past retained more strength in Central Asia and the Caucasus and among the indigenous peoples of Siberia. The Muslims and Christians of the Caucasus and the Muslims of

Central Asia even in the 1970s were more religious, more conservative, and more likely to be living in the countryside than Soviet citizens of European ancestry. Patriarchs still ruled the villages with a strong hand, and women remained enmeshed in ancient webs of dependency. They married at younger ages than women of European ancestry, divorced rarely, and had more children. They also enjoyed less formal education. When they moved to the cities, most went to join male relatives already there. Traditional customs such as bride price and wife beating continued, even though they were illegal and were prosecuted by Soviet authorities.

Naturally, the years of Soviet rule had brought change, particularly to the cities of Central Asia. The Party leadership, even after the disastrous Zhenotdel campaign of the 1920s, did not abandon its desire to undermine traditional society by emancipating women; but it did craft a more careful approach that depended on positive incentives and evolutionary change. Soviet citizens from the European areas were encouraged to move to the Caucasus and Central Asia, and millions did so, bringing their culture with them. Local people were offered education and jobs in the cities as a way out of the crushing poverty of traditional society. Once in the cities, of course, they imbibed the emancipatory values of Soviet-style modernization. This generally peaceful process brought about the transformation the government had wanted: by the 1970s, women in Baku, Tbilisi, Alma Ata, and Tashkent were educated, were working outside the home, and were professing many of the same ideas about family life and their role in society as were city women everywhere in the Soviet Union.

Very real cultural differences remained, however, because men still enforced their remaining prerogatives, and also because women labored to preserve those customs they particularly cherished. Uzbek women cooked in clay ovens built into the floors of their city houses, and bragged about the superiority of storing food in deep holes in the garden over putting them in expensive and unreliable Soviet refrigerators. Armenians taught their daughters centuries-old embroidery designs. The women of the Siberian peoples wore skirts and blouses to work, then changed into leather tunics and pants at home. All these women kept up the old, extended family ties to their kin in the cities and the countryside, even while themselves living in nuclear families. And they still worked for months to arrange feasts, particularly wedding feasts that drew together friends and family to celebrate in the old ways. Many women also preserved their religion; for years, Georgian and Armenian Christianity were practiced mostly by women, while female shamans on the Pacific coast still prayed to ancestral spirits for healing. Thus women kept alive some of the customs that had made them feel valuable in traditional society. They also nourished the several heritages of their once distinctly different societies.

THE ROLE OF GOVERNMENT, 1953–1982

All these developments in women's lives were affected by decisions made by the governments headed by Nikita Khrushchev (1956–1964) and Leonid Brezhnev (1964–1982). Stalin's successors were reformers, eager to foreswear the terror of the past, yet determined to preserve the Communist Party's monopoly on power. As reformers they were not interested in redefining the New Soviet Woman—the ideal of the 1930s had remained essentially unchanged—but they were willing to acknowledge how difficult it was for women to cope with all their duties, and they spent more money on programs beneficial to women. These efforts had limited success, though, because the politicians continued to favor heavy industry and the military over social services and consumer goods. They also refused to permit any critical re-examination of the fundamental principles on which the Soviet approach to women's emancipation was based.

The Khrushchev Years

Nikita Khrushchev was a flamboyant leader who liked extravagant gestures and folksy rhetoric. He cut the power of the police, created a freer climate for discussion within Soviet society, and opened up contacts with the outside world. Because he renounced terror as a method of government, he had to provide more positive incentives to motivate the Soviet people to work hard and support the Party. He experimented, developing one approach after another to raise the standard of living and decentralize the economy. Women as well as men figured in his calculations, for Khrushchev, like so many Russian reformers before him, saw women's situation as one of the reasons for Russia's backwardness.

Khrushchev never made women's issues a high priority, but he did promote some reforms beneficial to women. In 1955 abortion was again legalized, on the grounds that illegal abortions were damaging women's health. In the late 1950s the fees charged for divorce were lowered, thus making it more practicable for more people. The government also began enforcing protective labor laws, with the mixed results discussed above. But Khrushchev's most significant contribution may have been his reopening of discussion of the difficulties in women's lives, a discussion that had been halted in the early 1930s when Stalin's government had declared that women's emancipation was already fully realized.

The issue was framed in limited, reformist terms. Khrushchev and the politicians and propagandists who followed his lead maintained that while the Party had properly conceptualized women's emancipation, the country had not yet in fact achieved it. This was in part because of the country's continuing poverty, but it was also because individual men, many of them, were thwarting women's advancement by discriminating against them. The result, Khrushchev declared, was that very few women occupied leadership positions. He set out to create some role models. For example, in 1957 he appointed Ekaterina Furtseva, the minister of culture, to the Politburo, the first woman ever to serve on that body. As a result of a similar initiative, in 1963 cosmonaut Valentina Tereshkova became the first woman to orbit the earth.

More substantive than the exploits of these highly publicized women, however, was Khrushchev's authorization of the establishment of "women's soviets" (*zhensovety*). Enthusiastic promoters of these institutions hailed them as reincarnations, in miniature, of the Zhenotdel, and in fact there were strong similarities between the two organizations. Both consisted of a network of committees led by female communists. Both sought to enlist women in community-service projects and in campaigns to raise worker productivity. Both were charged as well with remedying the difficulties in women's lives, particularly those in the workplace that negatively affected productivity. Both were supposed to rely on women's volunteer labor. But the zhensovety were not to be, as the Zhenotdel had been, lobbies for women within the Party, and consequently they were organized only on the local or regional level, without any national leadership. Furthermore, their relationship to the Party was even more vaguely defined than the Zhenotdel's had been; it was not clear whether zhensovety were Party organizations or whether they were a sort of women's auxiliary attached to factories and offices. Furthermore, no zhensovety were established in Moscow or Leningrad, on the grounds that women's consciousness was already sufficiently high there. Rather they were concentrated in rural areas, smaller cities, and the non-European republics, far from the centers of power, where women could be expected not to use them as a platform for making loud complaints, or where, if they did, no one in the capitals would hear them.

The limited vision of the post-Stalin reformers is nowhere clearer than in the zhensovety. It was twenty-five years since the Zhenotdel had been abolished, and still the Party leaders were fearful of rousing feminism and alienating local Party leaders. Thus they designed the zhensovety to be so weak that they would be able to accomplish little more than industrial boosterism, a vague Soviet-style brand of spiritual uplift. An individual zhensovet, led by a committed, effective woman, might be able to mobilize the women of a factory or town to improve a day-care center or plant a flower bed. It might be able to expose the abuses of a factory manager, if it could win the support of other local, male bosses. But no volunteer organization of this sort could possibly remedy the fundamental economic and social problems that burdened women. The government must certainly have known this, so it is difficult to avoid the conclusion that it was simply trying once again to enlist female volunteers to deal with issues it did not want to spend money on. Many Soviet women saw the scheme for what it was worth, and they castigated the zhensovety as just another machine to exploit their labor.

The Brezhnev Years

Most of Khrushchev's efforts to overhaul the Soviet economy and political system proved just as ineffective as the zhensovety. In October 1964, the Party leaders, tired of his bombast, his barnyard wisdom, and his poorly planned reforms, forced him to resign, replacing him with a coalition led by Leonid Brezhnev. Brezhnev, a stone-faced Party functionary, in his triumph symbolized the dominance of the new ruling class, its cautious imperialism abroad, its love of order and stability at home, and its new vulnerability to imported delights such as Japanese televisions and Italian shoes.

Under Brezhnev the Politburo continued reformist activity, but prized restraint as Khrushchev had not, and also sought to introduce calm into a system so often in the past beset by upheaval. The new leadership greatly raised spending on the military but also invested more in agriculture. Wages improved; so did social benefits. To pay for all this, the government continued to underfund the consumer sector of the economy and responded to pent-up demand by permitting the growth of a black market in foreign-made clothing and electronics. It also sought foreign investment to pump up domestic production. Hence contacts between Soviet society and the outside world grew during the 1960s and 1970s. Brezhnev did not realize it, but in all these policies he was sewing the seeds of communist self-destruction.

Meanwhile, the women of the elite prospered. The special stores in which they shopped were piled high with imported goods as well as luxury Soviet products, sold at artificially low prices. Their children attended the best schools, and they could afford nice summer homes and even foreign travel. Meanwhile ordinary women across the U.S.S.R., ever more aware of the disparities between their lives and those of more privileged women at home and abroad, struggled with the difficulties of the double shift and scrounged for small amenities and pleasures which were taken for granted in Western Europe or the United States.

Government officials in the Brezhnev years continued from time to time to bemoan the problems women endured, though rather perfunctorily and without Khrushchev's flair for pointed remonstrances with male audiences. It is arguable, though, that Brezhnev's faceless bureaucrats accomplished more of benefit to women than Khrushchev's. With little fanfare they revised the marriage law in 1965 and 1968, simplifying divorce procedures and reducing fees still further. The 1968 marriage code also legalized community property and instituted no-fault divorce for couples with no children. (Childless couples could obtain a divorce without going to court if they agreed on the terms of the dissolution of their marriage. People with children still had to have court approval of their divorce and custody arrangements.)

The Brezhnev leadership also moved the discussion of women's situation into the universities. The 1960s saw the revival of social science, particularly sociology, in the U.S.S.R., and some sociologists and economists, many of them women, began to study the position of women in Soviet society. The government, anxious to find ways to increase the productivity of female workers, encouraged such studies. The result was a surge of books and articles, many based on public opinion surveys, that documented the double shift in considerable detail and called for increased funding for social services to relieve women's burdens.

This was the fullest discussion of these problems since the 1920s, but, publicly at least, the new social scientists did little more than call for greater relief from housework. Certainly they did not rethink the basic conceptions of the New Soviet Woman or reconsider the means to her emancipation. If anything, they stressed more forcefully than in the past women's nurturing responsibilities. While affirming as usual women's rights to full participation in the society, these academics and educators emphasized the importance of motherhood, declaring that it was women's nature to derive their primary satisfaction from domestic life. They justified this premise—officially approved since the 1930s—with pseudoscientific discussions of male and female personality that were practically neo-Victorian. Women, they declared, were emotional, dependent, and loving. Men, by contrast, were rational, aggressive, and primarily oriented toward the public world. Typical of such propaganda was this passage from a 1968 work on child-rearing by L. A. Levshin, a Soviet expert on education: "For woman it is natural to lean on the help, the support, and the protection of man, in order to give life to a new creature, rear him, and make him independent. And it is equally natural for the man to support, protect and defend the woman in order that she is able to fulfill the mission entrusted to her by nature."[5]

Such stereotyped views not only contradicted all the assertions that women were rightfully equal to men in Soviet society, they also ran directly counter to Soviet realities. Soviet women were not weak and dependent; they were in fact carrying the weight of the family on their broad backs. It seemed all the more unjust, therefore, when some of these same social scientists blamed the rising divorce rate, the catastrophic prevalence of male alcoholism, and, of course, juvenile delinquency on the fact that women were too absorbed in their jobs to be good mothers and wives.

It is true that social scientists throughout the European world often propagated such ideas about women and men in the postwar era, at least until feminism reemerged in the 1960s. Sociologists and psychologists in the United States, Britain, and France defined women as innately domestic and prophesied a host of disasters if wives put their individual aspirations ahead of their family responsibilities. In this the social scientists were only giving a scientific imprimatur to the belief widespread throughout the industrialized world that women's nurturance was crucial to maintaining social order. This vision of women had enjoyed broad support in the Soviet Union since the 1930s. In propagating it in the 1960s and 1970s, therefore, Soviet social scientists, like their counterparts in the West, were reflecting rather than analyzing the values of the society they studied.

Soviet academics worked, however, under far more direct ideological controls than did those in the West, and in the 1970s, Soviet political leaders instructed them to stress the importance of motherhood not simply because they believed in it, but also because the government was deeply concerned about the nation's falling birthrate. Social scientists accurately reported the truth: Soviet couples were having so few children because it was so hard to raise them in the cities. The government responded with propaganda designed to convince women that their emotional health depended on being mothers, and also

---

5 L. A. Levshin, *Mal'chik, muzhchina, otets* (Moscow, 1968), 13–14, quoted in Lynne Attwood, "The New Soviet Man and Woman—Soviet Views on Psychological Sex Differences," *Soviet Sisterhood*, edited by Barbara Holland (Bloomington, 1985), 66.

with material incentives: increasing the benefits paid to women on maternity leave, improving the pay for those taking time off to nurse sick children, and establishing welfare payments for children in low-income families. The program was a multifarious attempt to enhance childbearing in a female population that had learned to minimize life's chronic headaches by having only one child. Thus in the mid-1970s, regional commissions were established to investigate and publicize difficulties in women's lives. In the early 1980s, the government raised maternity benefits yet again and extended maternity leave to one year without loss of job seniority. At the same time, economists and politicians drafted proposals to create part-time jobs for women with young children.

Not all social scientists simply mouthed the conventional wisdom or did the government's bidding, however. There were some academics who resisted the pressure to champion motherhood and worked their way instead toward rethinking the fundamental premises of the Soviet program on women's emancipation. They began in the sixties and seventies by reaffirming the Marxist proposition that women had a right to independence that they could only realize by participation in the public world. In the early 1980s, a few scholars reexamined official thinking on domesticity as well, declaring that men should share housework with their wives and should also take a greater role in rearing the children. Some even criticized Marxist economics for not analyzing the contribution that domestic labor made to the nation's economy. These stirrings of discontent with Marxist orthodoxy and officially approved definitions of masculinity and femininity did not produce debates on women's situation nearly as vibrant and creative as those of the 1920s. In fact most of the arguments had been made, and made better, in the Zhenotdel press in the 1920s. Still, the cracks in Academe did indicate that the principles of Marxist feminism were still alive, and they presaged as well a revival of feminist ideas in the Gorbachev years.

Thus the Brezhnev era continued the discussions of the "woman question" that had begun under Khrushchev. Once again Russian intellectuals were considering what society should do for and about women. It was an analysis the policy-makers could not ignore, given their other priorities, but neither were they willing to permit it to go beyond the narrow, reformist boundaries they had erected for all discussions. The Brezhnev men were, in their own way, just as conservative as the tsars had been, just as wedded to the basic arrangements of power they had inherited and just as fearful of fundamental change. Yet like the tsars they too wanted a modern, productive economy run by well-trained workers, efficient managers, and creative intellectuals. They realized that this required loosening controls, not tightening them, but every time they permitted greater latitude to the citizenry, people on whose cooperation they depended began to act independently. Sociologists argued against the veneration of motherhood. Textile workers refused to have anything to do with the zhensovety. And in the late 1960s, small groups of intellectuals scattered all over the Soviet Union began to create what the foreign press quickly dubbed "the dissident movement."

The dissident movement grew out of the Brezhnev government's efforts to rein in free-thinking intellectuals. Its roots lay in the eased atmosphere of the Khrushchev period, but participants in the movement use the 1966 trial of two writers, Iulii Daniel and Andrei Siniavskii, to date the actual formation of an overtly political opposition. The writers were accused of anti-Soviet activities for publishing their books abroad without first obtaining official permission. A few of their friends took the daring and dangerous step of publicly defending them, and thereafter organized a loose network of people to circulate pamphlets and books that were critical of the Soviet status quo. This underground literature of typed manuscripts was christened *samizdat*, an acronym meaning "self-publishing." The government struck back by deporting or imprisoning the leading dissidents, and by the late 1970s had silenced most of them. But by then their calls for democracy, national self-determination, and an end to the Cold War had been heard by thousands, possibly tens of thousands of people, laying the foundations for the outburst of reform that was to startle the outside world after 1985. In fact, the dissidents were the first to use the word *glasnost* to mean freedom of speech and press.

Women were involved in the dissident movement from the beginning, primarily in support roles similar to those they had played in the revolutionary underground. They typed manuscripts, collected money and clothes for people in jail, and distributed literature. A number of them became prominent defenders of their jailed husbands. Elena Bonner, wife of physicist and human-rights activist Andrei Sakharov, was perhaps the best known. The works of female authors, particularly poet Anna Akhmatova and memoirists Nadezhda Mandelshtam and Evgenia Ginzburg, also figured importantly in samizdat literature. Yet despite the participation of women in every aspect of the dissident movement, male and female dissidents paid little attention to the special economic and social problems of women in Soviet society, being more absorbed by such issues as freedom of the press, the rule of law, religious freedom, and self-determination for the nationalities. Adopting the stance of the nineteenth-century revolutionaries who were their heroes, the dissidents declared that the important question was democratizing society.

And yet, like so many such general reform movements in the last two hundred years, this one did eventually produce people who devoted themselves to the improvement of women's situation—that is, feminists. In December 1979, a group of women in Leningrad, led by poets Tatiana Mamonova and Julia Voznesenskaia and philosopher Tatiana Goricheva, published a samizdat magazine, *Almanac: Woman and Russia*. In the first issue the editors proclaimed their intention to establish a forum wherein women could express their discontents and through this "get moving on women's liberation, on lightening women's lot."[6] The rest of the magazine was devoted to articles by professional women and blue-collar workers that documented in touching personal detail the hardships of Soviet women's lives. *Almanac* lasted a very short time, for the KGB [7] forced the editors to emigrate from the Soviet Union in 1980, but the appearance of this magazine was yet another portent of the development of more widespread feminist thinking under Gorbachev. Thus the Brezhnev years, for all their surface calm, generated the most critical analysis of the situation of women in Soviet society since the heyday of the Zhenotdel.

---

6 *Zhenshchina i Rossiia* (Paris, 1980), 124.

7 KGB stands for Committee for State Security, yet another name for the police agency responsible for political offenders. The KGB also dealt with espionage.

CONCLUSIONS

In the decades between the death of Stalin in 1953 and the death of Brezhnev in 1982, the Soviet Union became an urban, industrial society. As a consequence, the lives of most Soviet women came to resemble closely those of women elsewhere in the European industrialized world, and for many this marked a most dramatic improvement over the conditions under the tsars or in the early Soviet decades. Women continued to cope with many difficulties, however, because of the nation's enduring poverty and the choices made by its leaders.

In the late 1970s, the profound inefficiencies of the Soviet economic and political systems and the incompetence of the country's unimaginative and intransigent leadership slowed economic growth. Women bore the consequences of this stagnation as they stood in ever longer lines or coped with deteriorating housing and inadequate medical care. As their difficulties multiplied, so did their discontents. Thus the glow of women's considerable achievements in the postwar era had dimmed by 1985, when a new generation of men took over the leadership of the Communist Party.

6 / GLASNOST AND PERESTROIKA, 1985–1991

First Secretary of the Communist Party Leonid Brezhnev died in 1982. Three years later, in March 1985, after his two successors, Yuri Andropov and Constantine Chernenko, also died in office, a new generation of Party leaders came to power. They elected Mikhail Gorbachev First Secretary. Within a year his frank criticism of Soviet society and daring overtures in foreign policy were astonishing the outside world. Six years later, in 1991, the process of reform that Gorbachev launched swept him from power, and soon thereafter the Communist Party itself was abolished.

The parallels in these historic events to the revolution of 1917 were striking. Once again, as in the prerevolutionary period, a government in Russia had initiated and then tried to control major change. Once again it had failed because of economic and political mismanagement. Once again blue-collar workers and intellectuals had mounted the challenge to authority, but this time they were backed by a large middle class of professionals and white-collar workers. This time the government itself split, with reformers leaving it to set up the rival centers of power from which they eventually overthrew it.

Women played a role in this revolution comparable to their role in 1917. Again they took part in demonstrations and strikes and joined political organizations. But as in 1917 the leadership was overwhelmingly male, and power, when it was passed, moved from one coalition of men to another. Furthermore, as in 1917, women were divided in their opinions of what should be done to reform Soviet society. Feminism revived in the late 1980s, but there were many women, then as in 1917, who rejected any sort of public role and argued that women should concentrate their energies on their families. Meanwhile the economy continued to deteriorate alarmingly, making the lives of ordinary women more anxious and hectic, and turning them ever more into creatures whose main purpose in life, it seemed, was to stand in endless lines to buy basic commodities. As in 1917, their loud cries for relief were heard amidst the tumult.

THE GORBACHEV REFORMS

Many of the men who worked with Mikhail Gorbachev to reform the Soviet system had come of age under Khrushchev. They began with his basic idea—to make socialism succeed by democratizing politics and the economy. They formulated two slogans to describe their goals, *glasnost* and *perestroika*. *Glasnost*, a word that literally means "openness," signalled in practice a loosening of controls on intellectuals and the communications media in order to encourage criticism of the status quo and build support for reform. *Perestroika* was the slogan for economic restructuring, which included decentralization of economic management, experimentation with private ownership of small businesses, and encouragement of foreign investment.

There was resistance to reform from the very beginning, openly from conservative Party leaders, more covertly from factory and collective-farm managers, directors of scientific institutes, and many others whose encrusted power and privileges were threatened. Gorbachev headed a shifting coalition of reformers; as they encountered resistance, they pushed for more democracy and more freedom of expression in order to bring public pressure to bear on their opponents. Demonstrations and strikes were permitted. New political parties began to form. So too did independence movements in the non-Russian republics. By the spring of 1991, legislatures in the borderlands were challenging the Communist Party's hegemony and the Baltic states had begun to secede from the Soviet Union.

By then the Party leadership was deeply split between those who wanted to continue reform and those who wanted to curtail or reverse it. This conflict built to a crisis in August 1991, when a small group of Party leaders attempted to seize control by commanding military units in Moscow to arrest the reformers.

Most of the top military brass refused to act. Not so the parliament of the Russian republic. Led by its popular president Boris Yeltsin, it moved quickly and decisively and in three days forced the conspirators to back down. Gorbachev, who had been held captive throughout the attempted coup in his vacation home in the Crimea, returned to Moscow humbled and weakened by his association with the fallen conservatives. Soon he resigned as First Secretary of the Party. Yeltsin and the Russian parliament, emboldened by the coup's failure, banned the Communist Party and dismantled its central apparatus in September 1991. Also emboldened, leaders of those republics that had not already seceded from the Soviet Union rushed to do so in the autumn of 1991. The U.S.S.R. went to its own funeral in December 1991 when the presidents of the Russian, Ukrainian and Belorussian republics declared that the Soviet Union had been replaced by a loose alliance of independent republics entitled the Commonwealth of Independent States (C.I.S.).

Economic restructuring came more slowly than these whirlwind political changes, this collapse of the communist state. Gorbachev and his allies were more cautious in undertaking economic reform than they were in opening up the political process, both because of their continuing commitment to socialist ideals and because of their reluctance to set off the hardships that surely would come from dismantling the centralized system of production and distribution. Any system, however bad, was better than a completely disrupted one, which predictably would lead first to even emptier shelves, then to massive unemployment, followed by popular rage and unrest. Perhaps the reformers were also overwhelmed by the difficulty of transforming a centrally managed economy. They well knew that their economy worked very badly in contrast to the flourishing capitalism of Western Europe, North America, and East Asia, but which systems should they emulate, and at what speed? The reformers disagreed with one another on how to proceed as well as on what to proceed toward. Meanwhile the bureaucrats who ran the factories and ministries put obstacles in their way, and local officials bent on preserving their own prerogatives dug in their heels. Freed from the strong controls of the old system, the economy stumbled, so that by the end of the 1980s the gross national product and the standard of living were falling rapidly across the Soviet Union. For women, for all Soviet people, this meant ever longer lines, ever more hardship, anxiety, crime, discontent, and even emigration for those who could manage it.

The difficulties of women's lives were on the reform agenda of the Gorbachev years, as they had been on the special agendas of reformers in Russia since Peter the Great. Gorbachev himself, like Khrushchev, discussed them as an index of the shortcomings of the Soviet system and targeted them as something requiring great improvement. He also, again like Khrushchev, appointed a woman, Alexandra Biriukova, to the Politburo. But that was about it. As had so often been the case earlier, other issues were more important than women's problems. Since Gorbachev did not put them very high on the agenda, when it came to taking steps, his leadership fell back on the approaches of the Brezhnev era. The politicians authorized the creation of social-science study groups to consider women's problems, and they attempted to breathe life into the zhensovety by setting up a central leadership for them, the Soviet Women's Committee. This body did hold a national meeting of zhensovety delegates, the All-Union Conference of Women, in Moscow in 1987, at which speakers launched a broad critique of women's contemporary difficulties and singled out for particular attention men's monopoly on power. But by this time the Party leadership was so absorbed in the deepening economic and political crisis that they paid little attention.

WOMEN'S ATTITUDES TOWARD REFORM

As in the past, women reacted to political change as did many men of their own class, region, and ethnicity. Some elite women in the urban areas enthusiastically joined the reform cause; others became equally ardent defenders of the Communist Party's prerogatives. Some working-class women shrugged their shoulders and kept working, condemning the whole process as just another propaganda show; others shouted encouragement to their striking husbands. Women in the Baltics, Ukraine, and the Caucasus hearkened to the call of national independence, while peasants waited as usual to be shown that all the city talk was going to bring real improvements to the countryside.

Quickly, however, a distinctly female voice also emerged in the chorus of complaints. At first those who spoke up in the press and in polls were inclined to blame their problems on the abusive, domineering behavior of men and the corruption and incompetence of government leaders. "In general in this country we have so many problems!" said Olya, a seventeen-year-old vocational student interviewed in 1989. "Men don't want to face them, and they can't resolve them, and the women take everything upon themselves." To remedy the situation, women such as Olya wanted the government to spend more money on social services. They also demanded that women's rights be honored in the workplace. And they bemoaned the dismal economy, for they were tired of growing old coping with poverty. E. Frolova, A. Govorukhina, and N. Borisova, three women from Morshansk, a Russian provincial city, wrote to the magazine *Ogonyok* in 1987, "People who have been to Paris are ecstatic over the women there. They all look so young and elegant. In our opinion, the point is not the women themselves. How are you supposed to be young-looking when you're prematurely gray and there's no hair dye available to give your hair the right color?"[1] Soviet women did not know how many women in Western Europe and North America were also burdened with poverty and the double shift. They longed for comfort, rest, and respect and knew that most women in the United States or Western Europe had much more of all of these than they did.

As glasnost spread and women grew less cautious about speaking their minds publicly, their criticism grew more penetrating. Many declared that Soviet-style emancipation was a fraud, for it had not freed women, but rather had turned them into beasts of burden who worked under government command to fulfill government plans. Larisa Kuznetsova, a philologist, summed up the growing rejection of the Soviet status quo: "Women have

---

1 Deborah Adelman, *The "Children of Perestroika:" Moscow Teenagers Talk About Their Lives and the Future* (Armonk, NY, 1992), 74; *Small Fires: Letters from the Soviet People to Ogonyok Magazine 1987-1990*, ed. Christopher Cerf and Marina Albee (New York, 1990), 115.

been manipulated throughout most of our history. Put on tractors, or on steam engines, or dropped out of planes with parachutes. . . . Spiritual food and values have always been offered from without. From ready-made recipes. . . . We won't have any women's movement until women have the chance to stop this race, to concentrate on themselves, to understand and hear their own voices."[2]

Women did hear one another's voices as glasnost expanded. Some were raised in religious exaltation. Women all over the Soviet Union had kept Christianity alive since the Revolution, making up the overwhelming majority of parishioners through those years. In the late 1980s more and younger women began to practice the faith, justifying their conversions by arguing that religion permitted them to express their feminine spirituality in acts of devotion and charity. A small number of women took vows as Russian Orthodox nuns; groups of laywomen restored churches and organized local philanthropy in towns and cities across the Soviet Union. This back-to-the-Church movement was particularly strong in the Baltics, Ukraine, and Georgia, where religious faith (Lutheranism and Catholicism in the Baltics, Ukrainian Orthodoxy and the Uniate Church in Ukraine, Georgian Orthodoxy in Georgia) was mingled with nationalist feeling.

Other women, primarily educated ones from the Soviet Union's major cities, drew on sources of faith less ancient than Christianity. They took the idea that women were morally superior to men—an idea that they had been taught since childhood, an idea particularly strong in Russian culture since the intelligentsia had romanticized female revolutionaries in the nineteenth century—and made it their central principle. They argued that women were more loving, more sensitive, and less selfish than men. These qualities were the essential core of femininity (the "woman's principle" as the Federation of Women Writers put it). Freed from the burdens and restraints of Soviet life, they would beautify the family and society at large. Many of those who made this argument went on to assert that women should concentrate their energies on their families, and de-

2 Quoted by Nina Belyaeva, "Feminism in the USSR," *Soviet Women*, special issue of *Canadian Woman Studies, Le Cahiers de la Femme* 10, no. 9 (Winter 1989): 18.

manded that the government help them do so. Sociologist Tatiana Zaslavskaia, for instance, renewed the call, first heard in the Brezhnev years, for part-time jobs to be created so that mothers could spend more time with their children. Freedom, many women said, meant they should be able to choose not to work the double shift.

Women called for more time at home because they were simply exhausted from the daily grind. Many of them also wanted to turn their backs on the venality and incompetence of the falling communist government, on politics in general, and on involvement in the complex, uncontrollable world beyond the family. But in blaming the Communists for exploiting them over the years, they seemed unaware of the extent to which their problems were also a product of patriarchal institutions and traditions. In fact, those affirming feminine virtues seemed at first glance simply to be reiterating ideas about women and men that came straight out of patriarchal traditions. This was not unusual; people searching for something to believe in as society changes rapidly around them usually rely on their deepest articles of faith, and many Soviet women believed deeply in the nurturing qualities they had been taught to cultivate. Nor was this faith in their own virtues peculiarly Soviet or even neo-Victorian. Such faith also flourished among women, feminists as well as nonfeminists, in the United States and Western Europe in the late twentieth century. For example, it lay behind the oft-made assertion that female politicians would be more selfless, female soldiers more humane, than their male counterparts.

Some people in the crumbling U.S.S.R., most of them intellectuals in the big cities, accepted the concepts of female virtue but rejected the praise of domesticity. Rather they called for women to continue their participation in the public world but as men's equals. Women's problems would be solved, they argued, only by breaking down patriarchal values and male control over politics and economics, as well as by revolutionizing the family through the sharing of tasks and power between wives and husbands. These changes would make it possible for women's work outside the home to serve their needs and at the same time reform the society. Journalist Nina Belayeva sketched out this feminist plan for social regeneration in 1989, in terms that would have pleased both Kollontai and the Russian feminists Kollontai had so often criticized: "Though there are still no signs of a mass movement, the first women's associations have appeared. They will foster leaders, public figures, and politicians with a female face. Then women shall have a place in the social hierarchy worthy of our intellect, experience, education, and creativity. Women will occupy this place not by 'battling their way' into it, but by naturally imparting their womanhood upon society. Maybe then society will also understand that whenever women flourish, the nation stands to gain."[3]

The new Soviet feminists quickly contacted feminists abroad, trading ideas and setting up collaborative projects. By the early 1990s, a few academics were teaching and researching women's studies and gender studies, while writers organized to promote feminist ideas in literature. The very word "feminism" was recovering from the opprobrium it had suffered under Soviet rule and was even becoming a somewhat trendy label that a few women adopted proudly. It remained to be seen, however, whether the female intellectuals who breathed new life into Russian feminism in the 1990s could communicate it to the great mass of women more effectively than their predecessors several generations before.

And finally, female voices in the late 1980s cried out for national self-determination. Stirrings toward independence had been detected among the peoples of the borderlands since the dissident movement began in the 1960s. In the 1980s, they swelled into waves of nationalism that swept the Baltic states, the Caucasus, Ukraine, and Moldavia. Nationalist sentiment also grew in Central Asia and among ethnic minorities such as the Tatars and the Ossetians. Women were involved in all these movements, and they also joined the newly formed independence parties, the largest of which, Sajudis in Lithuania and Rukh in Ukraine, actively recruited them.

The female leaders of Rukh and Sajudis denied that they had any feminist intentions. Like the revolutionaries and nationalists of the nineteenth century, they denigrated feminism as narrow and self-interested and declared that they were dedicated to the general cause of their people's liberation. The new female nationalists differed from their revolutionary predecessors,

---

3 Ibid., 19.

VALENTINA
TERESHKOVA

Valentina Tereshkova was the first woman to fly in space. Little in her early life foretold such an achievement. Tereshkova was born on a collective farm in the Iaroslavl province of central Russia in 1937. After her father, a tractor driver, was killed in World War II, her mother moved into the city of Iaroslavl, where she became a textile worker. Tereshkova went to school in the city, then worked first in a tire factory, later in the textile mill with her mother.

Tereshkova discovered that she loved flying when she joined a parachuting club in 1959. In 1961, after Yuri Gagarin made the first space flight, she wrote a letter to the administrators of the Soviet space program, volunteering for cosmonaut training. Her timing was perfect, for the Soviet Union and the United States were then competing with one another in the so-called "space race," an important part of which was the rapid development of the "manned" space-flight program. All the U.S. astronauts

were men, so Soviet authorities decided that they could score points in world public opinion with female cosmonauts. Tereshkova and several other women were immediately accepted, then put through a rigorous training program that Tereshkova passed with flying colors. Less than two years after she had volunteered, she was ready.

On June 16, 1963, Tereshkova blasted off in a spaceship named Vostok VI. In the following three days she made a solo flight of 1.2 million miles, circling the Earth forty-eight times. A delighted Nikita Khrushchev pointed out that her flight was longer than that of all four of the U.S. astronauts who had flown to date, combined. So much for the "bourgeois" notion that women were the weaker sex, he concluded.

Tereshkova's first flight was also her last. She continued to work in the Soviet space program as an aeronautical engineer and attended the Zhukov Military Aviation Academy in the late 1960s, but most of her time was devoted to the task of being a celebrity and government spokesperson. She was named "Hero of the Soviet Union" and given the Order of Lenin, the Soviet Union's highest honors. A crater on the reverse side of the moon was named after her. She married fellow cosmonaut Andrian Nikolaev and when they had a daughter, the press made much of the fact that this was the first child of two space travellers. In 1968 she was appointed head of the Soviet Women's Committee, an organization designed to cultivate good relations with women's organizations abroad. This post allowed her to travel often, making speeches praising Soviet accomplishments.

Later in her life, Tereshkova's reputation in the Soviet Union was tarnished by this association with the discredited leadership of the Brezhnev era. In 1986, when the Women's Committee became the administrative body heading the zhensovety, Tereshkova was removed as chair. This was the end of her career as Soviet celebrity, but her fame as the first female cosmonaut remained secure.

however, in rejecting women's involvement in the public world. Picking up the theme so prevalent in the late 1980s, they affirmed the importance of domesticity for women, adding that in the home women would serve as restorers of Ukrainian or Lithuanian or the other native cultures suppressed by Soviet rule. Women should leave the paid labor force, therefore, in order to concentrate on educating their children to revere the national spirit and traditions.

It is ironic that the women most vocal in expressing these sentiments were the Lithuanians, who were also among the best educated, most affluent women of the Soviet Union. The women of the Caucasus and Central Asia, still far more closely attached both to domesticity and to native traditions, were hardly to be heard from in the late 1980s. This was to be expected, given the continuing power of men among the Muslim peoples. It was also to be expected that some of the women of Rukh and Sajudis would turn to feminism as national independence failed to solve women's problems, and as the new male leaders proved no more responsive than the Soviet ones had been.

WOMEN IN THE REFORM MOVEMENTS

Women reacted in different ways to the upheavals of the late 1980s. Some marched joyously in demonstrations, some continued to ardently support the Communist Party, some remained mired in their personal problems and avoided demonstrators and communists alike. Bearing these individual differences in mind, however, it is possible to make some generalizations about their participation, and to compare it to that which figured in the 1917 revolution.

What we find in both cases is that substantial political change did not lead to power-sharing between women and men. For example, women made up less than 10 percent of the delegates to the founding congress of Rukh in 1989. Nor were there many women in the new national and republican legislatures. For example, just 16 percent of the delegates in the Congress of People's Deputies elected in 1989 were women, and some of those were there because blocks of seats had been allocated to female communists and the zhensovety. Even lower percentages occurred in more democratically elected bodies such as the republican legislatures. Nor did the reform spirit encourage the great majority of Soviet people to rethink the enduring patriarchal idea that political leaders should be men. "It's just accepted here that a woman is a housewife, and politics is serious business, and the responsibility is great," declared Elena, a sixteen-year-old student from Moscow, in 1989.[4] When asked by pollsters in 1989 and 1990 whether they would vote for a female candidate, many Soviet people, including substantial numbers of women, answered that they would not. After all, they declared, Soviet female legislators had disgraced themselves in the past by rubber-stamping everything the leaders proposed. That men had behaved the same way did not seem to shake the widespread conviction that women in general were incapable of political leadership.

Consequently there were only a few female leaders in the reform movement. The first prime minister of independent Lithuania was a woman, Kazimera Prunskene. One of the earliest ideologists of glasnost was sociologist Tatiana Zaslavskaia; in the late 1980s she served as a delegate to the Russian parliament. Women were also active among conservatives. The best known was a Leningrad teacher and communist, Nina Andreeva, who first came to fame in the spring of 1988 when her letter criticizing perestroika was published in the party newspaper *Sovetskaia Rossiia*. After the August Coup she became a leader among those attempting to rebuild the Communist Party. Many less famous women worked in all sorts of political organizations spanning the political spectrum, but the great majority of the leaders and of rank-and-file members were men.

There were those who spoke out against this situation. Journalists criticized the fact that there were so few women in the new legislatures. The Soviet Women's Committee argued that quotas for female representation should be established, so as to increase women's participation. Such proposals found few supporters, however, for the quotas smacked too much of discredited Soviet tokenism.

Women did participate in political life in the late 1980s, even though, as in 1917, most remained outside political parties. They voted in large numbers for reform candidates; Boris Yeltsin, for

---

4 Adelman, *Children of Perestroika*, 172.

one, claimed to have drawn much of his early support from Moscow women. Women also took an active part in the same sorts of episodic, short-lived events—petitioning, riots, demonstrations, and strikes—that had been their forte in 1917. Many women marched for political reform in the major cities. Working-class women supported striking miners in Siberia and the Donets Basin. As in 1917, a few strikes were organized by women alone; in 1989, for example, female transport workers struck to protest the government's announcement of layoffs. Women also were active in the resistance to the August Coup: young women joined the young men ringing the headquarters of the Russian parliament while older women remonstrated with the soldiers occupying Moscow streets.

Women worked as well in the many volunteer organizations, some exclusively female, that sprang up with glasnost. The smaller women's groups were usually confined to a single city, where they pursued all sorts of projects—philanthropy, religious study, historic preservation, local arts and crafts. There were also larger organizations, such as the Committee of Soldiers' Mothers that lobbied in Moscow and Leningrad for increased veterans' benefits for their sons, and similar groups in Georgia and Ukraine that demonstrated against young men being sent to do military service outside their home republics. Memorial, the organization that investigated and publicized the atrocities of the Stalin era, had many female members. Within the professional community, academics and writers formed all-female organizations to promote contacts in Western Europe and North America, as well as to press their claims for recognition and funding. All this voluntarism added up to the highest levels of independent organizing by women since the Revolution.

THE CONSEQUENCES OF REFORM

The Soviet Union limped off into history in the fall of 1991, leaving behind a dismembered empire and a tottering economy. It had been born as angry women stood in lines; when it died, they were still standing, and they were still angry. How the new order would deal with their problems and what women's role would be in it were no clearer in 1991 than they had been in 1917. Political power remained in the hands of men, but this was hardly surprising. More troubling was the fact that none of the political parties that emerged in the successor states of the former Soviet Union gave women's situation a prominent place on its agenda.

Economic developments were equally alarming. More ineptly managed than ever, the economy deteriorated, and women spent more and more time every day standing in line for eggs or searching for baby clothes and diapers. The shortages of food and consumer goods were burdensome enough, but then female unemployment began to rise. Those engineering the transition to a market economy in Russia and the other nations of the former Soviet Union agreed that they must move workers out of heavy industry and into the critically inadequate consumer and service sectors. They agreed as well that they must cut the size of the government bureaucracy. All this required laying people off, a process that began in the late 1980s. Once again, as in the 1920s, the great majority of those let go were women. According to some estimates, twice as many women as men had lost their jobs by 1991, and although few of the authorities would admit it, it was clear that at least some of these layoffs were the result of discrimination against women.

The rising rates of female unemployment alarmed many people. Without a substantial improvement in the economy, many women could not afford to leave their jobs, even if they wanted to. Nor would most husbands, dependent on their wives' income, wish them to. There were also widespread fears that efforts to scale back government spending would lead to deep cuts in social-welfare programs and maternity benefits. Thus the prospect of tens of thousands of unemployed women and the possibility of even less adequate social programs aroused considerable anxiety in the early 1990s throughout the former Soviet Union, among men as well as women.

Nor were the Western influences flowing into the country uniformly beneficial. Some of the foreign companies that began doing business in Russia and the other republics of the C.I.S. openly discriminated against women in hiring and promotion. Feminism spread among intellectuals, but meanwhile the mass media burgeoned with images of women that ranged from demeaning to vilely exploitative. Advertising associated pretty, well-dressed, sexy young women with success, and in the process deepened illusions about women in the West. Filmmakers, copying their American counterparts, made violence against women a stock motif. Newly legalized pornography appeared on the streets. None of this would have been tolerated by the communist government, which had always denounced the selling of sex as degrading to women. Nor would that government have stood idly by when prostitutes began freely roaming the lobbies of the major hotels and young women lined up in the cold to register for work as strippers in privately owned restaurants.

The reforms of the 1980s did produce important changes that boded well for women, however. Of primary importance was the fact that Gorbachev and his successors sought to free up resources for the civilian economy by cutting military spending and drastically scaling back the Soviet Union's foreign commitments. For the first time since Peter the Great, Russia's leaders tried not to bankrupt the government by devoting millions of rubles to the pursuit of international power. For the first time they addressed themselves first and foremost to improving people's standard of living. This unprecedented reordering of priorities stood to benefit women in the long run by relieving the burdens of the double shift.

Women could also draw support from the very Soviet legacy so many of them criticized. Over the seventy years of its rule, the Communist Party had asserted the importance of women's equality and had legitimated women's concerns by putting them on the agenda. The result in the early 1990s in most of the successor states of the Soviet Union was widespread acceptance of women's basic social, legal, and political rights, as well as of the social programs they depended upon. Furthermore women were well educated in the early 1990s and far more used to speaking up to defend themselves than women had been in 1917. Contacts with Western women were growing, and although Western feminism brought with it no panaceas, it made available to the women of the former Soviet Union a rich body of ideas to draw on in formulating solutions. At the end of the twentieth century, the women of the former Soviet Union were far better prepared than their peasant grandmothers had been to benefit from, and defend themselves from, their nations' ongoing changes.

EPILOGUE

June 11, 1993, was a sunny day in Moscow, one of the few that cool, rainy summer. The sky cleared early, and the sun grew warm enough to make it uncomfortable when people crowded together in a bakery in a quiet, relatively prosperous residential neighborhood near the city center. It was also warm enough to make the old woman who crowded in with the rest stand out, for she was wearing a threadbare winter coat, heavy knitted stockings, and bedroom slippers. She had pulled her scarf low on her forehead, but even so the bruises on her left temple stood out, an ugly lavender and yellow against the translucent whiteness of her skin.

It was Friday, and people were lining up to buy bread for the weekend. In the way of most Soviet stores, this one had only one narrow door, through which the customers pushed and shoved. Inside there was barely room to move, but the old woman was used to crowds, and she was small and very thin, so she made her way quickly to the front of the line. She was entitled to go ahead because she was old. The cashier, a stout, efficient, middle-aged woman with iron-gray hair, was working quickly to relieve the crush. She did not look up as the customers gave their orders, but kept her eyes fixed on the cash register and called out the prices as she made change. The old woman told the cashier that she wanted one loaf of bread, then added angrily, "I've only had bread to eat this month." The cashier looked up at that, saw the coat, the slippers, and the bruises, shook her head sympathetically, gave the old woman her small change and receipt, and then began to declare loudly, over and over, as she hammered the register keys, "It is terrible to live alone, it is terrible to live alone, it is terrible to live alone." The other women waiting there shook their heads too, as the old woman pushed her way between them to get to the bins of fresh bread.

Everyone in the store—the well-dressed professionals in line, the bakery workers in white coats, the chanting cashier—they all knew that the ravaging inflation of the early 1990s, brought

SOFIA IVANOVNA
IURKOVA

Sofia Ivanovna Iurkova was a short, stout, white-haired cleaning lady in Moscow in the early 1990s. For cleaning two floors of a dormitory every day she received the equivalent of $10 per month, a necessary supplement to her government pension, but still barely enough to cover the cost of food. So Sofia Ivanovna did the laundry of the dormitory residents and worked weekends and holidays to earn a little extra.

Most days she came to work at 8 A.M., carrying the night's work in two large bags, and left at 6 P.M., her bags again almost full. On the way home she stopped off to buy groceries. Once home, she cooked the family dinner for her daughter, son-in-law, and granddaughter. Then she washed the jeans, shirts, and underwear she had brought home, hung them in the kitchen to dry, and sat down beside them to watch television. Only when the rest of the family had gone to sleep in

the apartment's one bedroom could Sofia Ivanovna lie down on her bed, the living room couch.

Seventy years old in 1993, Sofia Ivanovna was used to hardship. She had grown up in the deprivation of Moscow in the 1920s and 30s. So deep was her attachment to her father, a blue-collar worker, that when he was called up for military service in World War II, she volunteered so they would not be separated. The war took them away from one another despite her best efforts, but Sofia Ivanovna's strength and a lot of luck got her through all the days without food and the endless walking and the dangers of her assignment as an antiaircraft gunner. Her father died at the front only six days before the war ended in 1945.

After the war Sofia Ivanovna married, reared her daughter while working at various jobs, and was then widowed. With little education, she could not manage to escape the drudgery of

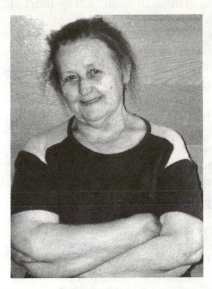

manual labor and could expect to work long after many women would have retired. Her pension was simply too small to live on.

Sofia Ivanovna was a cheerful person who believed in making the best of things. She took care to dress nicely every morning, even though she had to change into work clothes once she got to the dormitory. She filled her workroom there with singing birds and decorated the halls with beautiful houseplants, lovingly tended. Each day she collected the stale bread that the wasteful foreigners in the dormitory threw away, then dried it and fed it to the birds and to neighborhood cats and dogs. She took care of the foreigners with the same gentle solicitude, passing on tips to help them cope with Russian life and life in general. A devotee of folk medicine, Sofia Ivanovna taught her wards about Tibetan ways of treating disease and advised them to take no pills except American aspirin. She noticed when their beds had not been slept in. When they went home, she tearfully kissed them all goodby.

Yet for all her strengths, Sofia Ivanovna did not accept her situation happily. There was simply too much "foolishness" in Russians' lives, she declared, shaking her head sadly. She was particularly unhappy about the tiny apartment her family had to live in, where no one had any privacy. Still, in 1993 Sofia Ivanovna thought she was fortunate to have outlived the Soviet Union; she hoped that she would also live long enough to see everyday life become less arduous and less "foolish."

on by the government's clumsy efforts to build a free-market economy, had reduced many old women to destitution. It was not clear how many were not surviving, how many were being abandoned by their children, how many were dying because they could afford only bread. It was only certain that there were many poor old women in the rainy streets of Moscow in the summer of 1993, and that their evident misery bore in upon those more fortunate the graphic lesson that for a woman it was still "terrible to live alone."

And yet there were other women in Moscow in the early summer of 1993 who had reaped handsome rewards from the new Russian revolution. Now the shops, particularly those owned by foreign companies, and the kiosks lining all the major streets were full of consumer goods. The sidewalks teemed with fruit-and-vegetable vendors selling everything from Syrian eggplants to Crimean grapes. Bananas had been rare in Russia in the past; now yellow peels spilled out of trashcans all over town. These imports were far too expensive for most people, but the young women who worked for Siemens, Lever, Pepsico and the many other foreign companies active in the city earned good incomes, on average ten times what Russian employers paid, so they could afford French cosmetics and American clothes. Like most Russians they still grew a lot of their own food in country gardens, then canned or preserved it for the winter. Once in a while, however, they could have dinner at McDonald's, then buy a banana or a kiwi or a bag of German candy for dessert. These women smiled a lot as they walked down Tverskaia Street with their arms around their boyfriends, and their well-being shone in the summer evenings.

Most of the women of Russia and the other nations that had once been the Soviet Union were neither very old and desperate nor very young and fortunate in June of 1993. What they did with those days depended on who and where they were. In Minsk, Belorussia, a doctor spent the weekend picking and canning strawberries, then exchanging them with her sisters for asparagus, sweet peas, and more advice than she really wanted on the need to invest in newly privatized factories. In Donets, Ukraine, a clerk in a mining company organized a strike to protest miserable wages and awful working conditions. In Baku, Azerbaidzhan, friends talked worriedly about whether the new coup would

lead to street fighting. In Kazan, capital of the Tatar Autono-
mous Region, Tatar women and Russian women nodded pleas-
antly to each other in the streets and hoped that they could
preserve the spirit of mutual toleration in their city against the
ethnic animosities that were tearing so many republics of the
former Soviet Union apart. In Vladivostok, Siberia, a telephone
operator stood on the sidewalk late into the evening, offering
mended plastic raincoats and sandals from China for sale. In
Palekh, Russia, women artists dipped their brushes into glow-
ing pots of red and blue and gold and painted Russia's fairy tales
onto the small, jewel-like lacquer boxes prized by collectors
around the world.

All these women were strangers to one another, and the dis-
tances that separated them are a reminder of the enormous
diversity of experience that is obscured by generalizations about
the women of an entire nation. Nonetheless, they did possess
a common heritage. They shared a legacy of major strides in
education and employment, as well as in political and legal rights.
They kept alive powerful ideas about women that blended the
beliefs of their ancestors with more recent hopes for freedom
and equality. And, two years after the collapse of communism,
all but the most fortunate of them still set out every day, shopping
bags in hand, to cope with their nation's continuing, indeed,
worsening poverty.

In the summer of 1993, as Russia's strange, creeping, late-
century revolution continued to spin out liberation in politics
and the press, rampant corruption and inflation, government
bungling and economic decline, women all over what had been
the Soviet Union reaffirmed their faith in the ability to cope that
had sustained so many of them through all the catastrophes and
triumphs of Soviet history. Tamara Khripunova, a forty-eight-
year-old dentist in St. Petersburg, a pretty blonde woman with
bright blue eyes, put it this way: "We are used to hard times. It's
going to take decades for Russia to catch up with Western Europe. But we can wait. We're used to waiting. We'd like bigger
apartments, we'd like more appliances. I'd like better equipment
at work. We'd like more women in the legislatures. We'd like
men to treat us better. But we can wait. We're used to it."[1]

---

1 Personal communication, May 31, 1993.

APPENDIX

Table 1 **Women in the Population of the U.S.S.R.**

Number of Women (in 1000s and as a percentage of the population)

Year	1939	1959	1970	1985
Entire U.S.S.R.	99,273(52%)	114,777(55%)	130,321(54%)	146,682(53%)
Predominantly Slavic Republics				
Belorussia	4,595(52%)	4,475(56%)	4,864(54%)	5,296(53%)
Russia	57,276(53%)	65,109(55%)	70,754(54%)	76,646(54%)
Ukraine	21,107(52%)	23,294(56%)	25,821(55%)	27,434(54%)
Baltics				
Estonia	563(53%)	672(56%)	736(54%)	817(53%)
Latvia	998(53%)	1,174(56%)	1,283(54%)	1,397(54%)
Lithuania	1,499(52%)	1,466(54%)	1,660(53%)	1,887(53%)
Caucasus				
Armenia	634(49%)	921(52%)	1,275(51%)	1,695(51%)
Azerbaidzhan	1,562(49%)	1,941(52%)	2,634(51%)	3,384(51%)
Georgia	1,775(50%)	2,179(54%)	2,484(53%)	2,745(53%)
Central Asia				
Kazakhstan	2,920(48%)	4,880(53%)	6,746(52%)	8,178(52%)
Kirghizia	716(49%)	1,091(53%)	1,532(52%)	2,029(51%)
Tadzhikistan	715(48%)	1,016(51%)	1,474(51%)	2,274(51%)
Turkmenia	607(48%)	786(52%)	1,096(51%)	1,617(51%)
Uzbekistan	3,069(48%)	4,222(52%)	6,055(51%)	9,121(51%)
Moldavia	1,237(50%)	1,551(54%)	1,907(53%)	2,162(53%)

Source: "Zhenshchiny v SSSR," *Vestnik statistiki*, no. 1 (1986): 51.

Chart 1	Sex Ratios in the Soviet Population

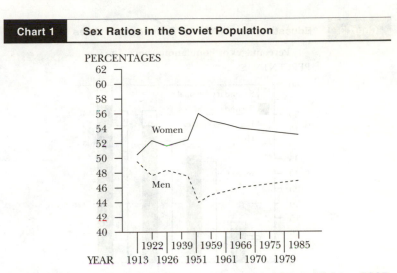

Adapted from Tsentral'noe Statisticheskoe Upravlenie pri Sovete Ministrov SSSR, *Zhenshchiny v SSSR* (Moscow, 1975), 9; "Zhenshchiny v SSSR," *Vestnik statistiki,* no. 1 (1986): 51

Chart 2	Growth in Literacy of Soviet Females

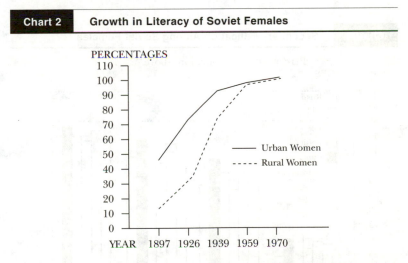

Includes all females age 49 and younger. Various definitions of literacy have been used by Soviet census-takers over the decades, calling the reliability and comparability of their findings into question. All the definitions, however, included at least the ability to read and write at a rudimentary level.

Adapted from Tsentral'noe Statisticheskoe Upravlenie pri Sovete Ministrov SSSR, *Zhenshchiny v SSSR* (Moscow, 1975), 55.

Chart 3   **Education Among Soviet Females and Males**

Percentages of Population Above Age 9
PERCENTAGES

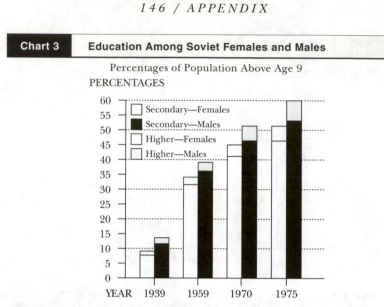

Adapted from Tsentral'noe Statisticheskoe Upravlenie pri Sovete Ministrov SSSR, *Zhenshchiny v SSSR* (Moscow, 1975), 61.

Chart 4   **Secondary Education Among Soviet Females**

Percentages of Population Above Age 10
PERCENTAGES

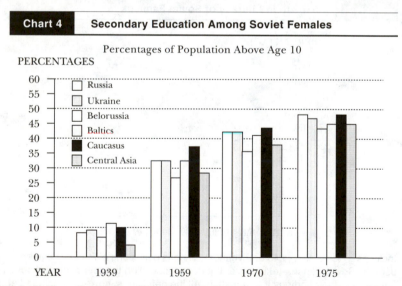

Adapted from Tsentral'noe Statisticheskoe Upravlenie pri Sovete Ministrov SSSR, *Zhenshchiny v SSSR* (Moscow, 1975), 62.

Chart 5	Employed Women As a Percentage of the Soviet Paid Labor Force

PERCENTAGES

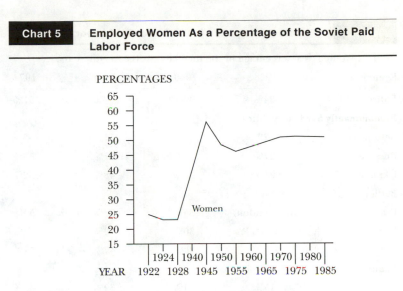

Adapted from Tsentral'noe Statisticheskoe Upravlenie pri Sovete Ministrov SSSR, *Zhenshchiny v SSSR* (Moscow, 1975), 27; "Zhenshchiny v SSSR," *Vestnik statistiki*, no. 1 (1986): 53.

Table 2	Female Participation in the Soviet Paid Labor Force			
	Women as a percentage of the total labor force for the years:			
Region	1928	1940	1965	1974
Entire U.S.S.R.	24%	39%	49%	51%
Predominantly Slavic Republics				
Belorussia	22%	40%	51%	53%
Russia	27%	41%	51%	53%
Ukraine	21%	37%	48%	52%
Baltics				
Estonia	Independent	35%	52%	54%
Latvia	of U.S.S.R.	36%	52%	54%
Lithuania		30%	47%	51%
Caucasus				
Armenia	15%	34%	39%	45%
Azerbaidzhan	14%	34%	40%	42%
Georgia	19%	35%	42%	45%
Central Asia				
Kazakhstan	15%	30%	42%	48%
Kirghizia	11%	29%	44%	48%
Tadzhikistan	7%	29%	38%	39%
Turkmenia	25%	36%	39%	40%
Uzbekistan	18%	31%	40%	42%
Moldavia	21%	35%	48%	52%

These figures include all women working as blue- and white-collar workers except those on *kolkozy* (collective farms).

Source: Tsentral'noe Statisticheskoe Upravlenie pri Sovete Ministrov SSSR, *Zhenshchiny v SSSR* (Moscow, 1975), 35.

Chart 6	Distribution of Females in the Soviet Paid Labor Force: Blue-Collar and White-Collar Workers

a. Percentages of All Employed Women

PERCENTAGES

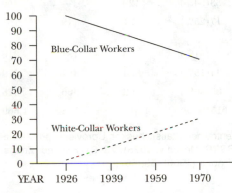

b. Percentages of All Workers in Each Category

PERCENTAGES

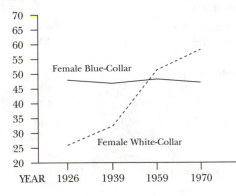

Adapted from Tsentral'noe Statisticheskoe Upravlenie pri Sovete Ministrov SSSR, *Zhenshchiny v SSSR* (Moscow, 1975), 27.

Table 3	Women in the Soviet Professions

Number of Women (in thousands and as percentage
of profession in 1941 and 1974)

	1941	1960	1965	1970	1974
Academics	33(34%)	129	—	360	465(40%)
Agronomists, veterinarians	17(25%)	91	119	157	179(38%)
Economists	18(31%)	113	181	316	422(65%)
Engineers	44(15%)	324	487	779	1,043(33%)
Physicians	85(60%)	302	366	428	486(70%)
Teachers	615(60%)	1,312	1,558	1,669	1,706(71%)

Adapted from Tsentral'noe Statisticheskoe Upravlenie pri Sovete Ministrov SSSR, *Zhenshchiny v SSSR* (Moscow, 1975), 78, 81, 86; and "Zhenshchiny v SSSR," *Vestnik statistiki*, no. 1 (1986): 55, 56.

Table 4	Family Life in the Soviet Union and the United States, 1965–1990

a. Family Demographics

Age at First Marriage (1990)	*Women*	*Men*
U.S.	23	25
U.S.S.R.	22	24

Average Household Size (persons)	*1970*	*1980s*
U.S.	3.1	2.7
U.S.S.R.	3.7	4.0

Fertility Rate (births per woman)	*1970*	*1990*
U.S.	2.6	1.8
U.S.S.R.	2.4	2.4

Women Currently Married (1990)	*Age 15–19*	*Age 25+*
U.S.	5%	57%
U.S.S.R.	9%	57%

Women Age 25–44 Currently Divorced (1990)		
U.S.	11%	
U.S.S.R.	9%	

Women over 60 Not Currently Married (1990)		
U.S.	59%	
U.S.S.R.	71%	

Table 4	Family Life in the Soviet Union and the United States, 1965–1990 (Continued)

b. Time Use   Expressed in hours per week

	U.S.		U.S.S.R.	
	Women	Men	Women	Men
Paid work				
1965	18.7	48.3	43	53.2
1986	24.5	41.3	38.5	49
Household chores				
1965	32.1	8.8	32.3	14
1986	29.9	17.4	25.7	14.6
Child care				
1965	5.7	1.3	3.6	1.4
1986	2	0.8	4.4	1.5
Total unpaid housework				
1965	37.8	10	35.9	15.4
1986	31.9	18.1	30.1	16.1
Personal care and free time				
1965	111	109	89	99
1986	112	109	99	103

Source: United Nations, Department of International Economic and Social Affairs, Statistical Office, *The World's Women, 1970–1990, Trends and Statistics* (New York, 1991), 26, 101.

Chart 7	Soviet Birth Rate

Live Births Per Thousand People in the Population
PERCENTAGES

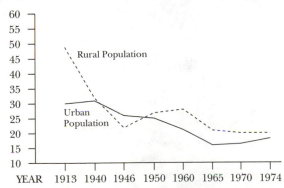

Adapted from Tsentral'noe Statisticheskoe Upravlenie pri Sovete Ministrov SSSR, *Zhenshchiny v SSSR* (Moscow, 1975), 101.

| Table 5 | Nuclear Family Size in the U.S.S.R., 1972 | | | | |

Percentages of families having 1 or more children under age 16

	1 child	2	3	4	5+
Entire U.S.S.R.					
Urban	58	34	6	2	1
Rural	38	33	15	7	7
Predominantly Slavic Republics					
Belorussia					
Urban	55	39	6	.7	.1
Rural	38	35	19	6	3
Russia					
Urban	62	33	4	.8	.3
Rural	43	36	14	5	3.5
Ukraine					
Urban	61	35	3	.4	.1
Rural	48	39	10.5	2	.8
Baltics					
Estonia					
Urban	60	35	3	1	.2
Rural	46.5	35	14	4	.3
Latvia					
Urban	66	30	3	.3	.3
Rural	52	36	9	2	2
Lithuania					
Urban	58	34	6	1	.5
Rural	38	38	16	6.5	2
Caucasus					
Armenia					
Urban	32	35	21	9.5	2
Rural	21	21	25.5	20	13
Azerbaidzhan					
Urban	36	33	15	9	7
Rural	13	17	16	18	36
Georgia					
Urban	42	42	13	2.5	.6
Rural	34	38	16	8	4

Table 5	Nuclear Family Size in the U.S.S.R., 1972 (Continued)

Percentages of families having 1 or more children under age 16

	1 child	2	3	4	5+
Central Asia					
Kazakhstan					
Urban	46	37	10	3	3
Rural	28	27	20	11	13
Kirghizia					
Urban	43	34	11	5.5	6.5
Rural	26	26	16	13	19.5
Tadzhikistan					
Urban	34	31	13	9	13
Rural	17	22	13.5	15	32
Turkmenia					
Urban	35	27.5	13	9	15.5
Rural	19	18	17	17	29
Uzbekistan					
Urban	38	29	14	9	11
Rural	21	18	18	17	26
Moldavia					
Urban	60	34	5	1	.4
Rural	43	31	14	7.5	5

Some rows total more or less than 100% because of rounding off of fractions.

Source: Tsentral'noe Statisticheskoe Upravlenie pri Sovete Ministrov SSSR, *Zhenshchiny v SSSR* (Moscow, 1975), 92–95.

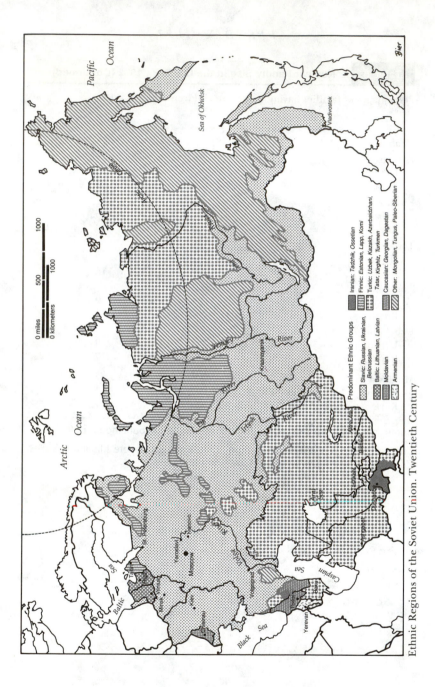

Ethnic Regions of the Soviet Union. Twentieth Century

Predominant Ethnic Groups

Slavic: Russian, Ukrainian, Belorussian
Baltic: Lithuanian, Latvian
Moldavian
Armenian

Iranian: Tadzhik, Ossetian
Finnic: Estonian, Lapp, Komi
Turkic: Uzbek, Kazakh, Azerbaidzhani, Tatar, Kirghiz, Turkmen
Caucasian: Georgian, Dagestan
Other: Mongolian, Tungus, Paleo-Siberian

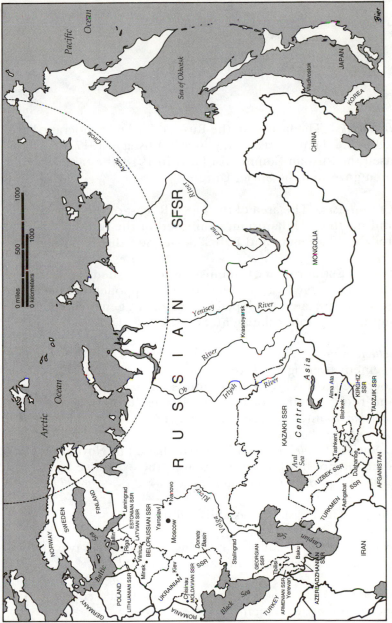

The Soviet Union, mid-1980s

Map labels:

Pacific Ocean

Sea of Okhotsk

Arctic Circle

SFSR

RUSSIAN

Arctic Ocean

Yenisey River

Lena River

Krasnoyarsk

Ob River

Irtysh River

River

CHINA

MONGOLIA

JAPAN

KOREA

Vladivostok

Bering

Central Asia

KAZAKH SSR

Aral Sea

UZBEK SSR

Alma Ata

Bishkek

KIRGHIZ SSR

TADZJIK SSR

Tashkent

Dushanbe

TURKMEN SSR

Ashgabat

AFGANISTAN

IRAN

Caspian Sea

Baku

AZERBADZHANIAN SSR

Yerevan

ARMENIAN SSR

Tbilisi

GEORGIAN SSR

TURKEY

Black Sea

Volga River

Stalingrad

Donets Basin

Moscow

Ivanovo

Yaroslavl

Kiev

UKRAINIAN SSR

MOLDAVIAN SSR

Chisinau

ROMANIA

POLAND

Minsk

BELORUSSIAN SSR

Vilnius

LITHUANIAN SSR

Riga

LATVIAN SSR

Tallinn

ESTONIAN SSR

Leningrad

FINLAND

Baltic Sea

SWEDEN

NORWAY

GERMANY

Scale:
0 miles   500   1000
0 kilometers   1000

GLOSSARY

Bolsheviks   The faction of the Russian Social-Democratic Party led by V. I. Lenin that seized power in Russia in 1917. Renaming itself the Russian Communist Party in 1918, it established and then governed the Soviet Union.

Central Asia   The area of the U.S.S.R. east of the Caspian Sea and north of Afghanistan, composed of the Kazakh, Kirghiz, Tadzhik, Turkmen, and Uzbek Soviet Socialist Republics.

Cheka   Extraordinary Commission; established in December 1917 and charged with arresting political opponents of the Soviet government; later developed into a police agency charged with suppressing political dissent. See also NKVD, KGB.

collectivization   The establishment of central government management over agriculture in the late 1920s and 1930s. This coercive process involved the confiscation of peasant property and reorganization of peasant villages into collective farms (*kolkhozy*) and state farms (*sovkhozy*).

Council of People's Commissars   Established in November 1917 after the Bolshevik seizure of power; the executive leadership of the first Soviet government.

Duma   The legislature established in 1906.

extended family   A family consisting of more than two generations living together in the same household.

feminism   The advocacy of women's political, economic, and social equality with men.

Five-Year Plans   The national plans for managing the Soviet economy.

glasnost   Literally, "openness"; refers to the freeing of press and public expression after 1985.

GULAG   The acronymic name of the Soviet agency in charge of forced-labor camps; refers to the entire forced-labor system.

KGB   Committee for State Security; the post-Stalin agency charged with controlling political dissent and espionage. See also Cheka.

Mensheviks   The larger faction of the Russian Social-Democratic Party in the prerevolutionary period.

modernization   The transformation of rural societies dependent on subsistence agriculture into urban societies chiefly dependent on industrialized production.

NEP   New Economic Policy, economic reforms initiated in 1921 that permitted some private enterprise. NEP also refers to the atmosphere of experimentation that prevailed in the 1920s.

NKVD   People's Commissariat of Internal Affairs, the political police that carried out the mass repressions of the Stalin era.

nuclear family   A family form based on parents and minor children living together in one household.

patriarchy   A set of political and social values based on the principle that power rightfully resides in the senior male heads of families.

perestroika   Literally, "rebuilding"; refers to the processes of economic reform launched by Gorbachev's government after 1985.

Provisional Government   The temporary government established in March 1917 to govern until a constituent assembly could write a constitution; overthrown by the Bolsheviks in October.

Russian Social-Democratic Labor Party (SDs)   The Marxist revolutionary party established in the 1890s; split in 1903 into Mensheviks and Bolsheviks.

samizdat   Literally, an acronym meaning "self-publishing"; refers to the fictional and nonfictional works circulated in typescript copies in the late 1960s and throughout the 1970s.

socialism   A philosophy that advocates the ownership and control of the economy (industry, natural resources, and capital) by the community as a whole.

Socialist Revolutionary Party (SRs)   The party established in Russia in the early 1900s. Although greatly influenced by Marxism, its members built support among peasants as well as workers.

Soviets   Originally established in 1917 as elected bodies representative of workers, soldiers, and peasants. After the Bolsheviks seized power, they transformed them into the legislative branch of their new government.

Stakhanovites   Highly productive workers who were held up as models by the government in the 1930s and 1940s. The name refers to the first such exemplary worker, A. G. Stakhanov.

Zhenotdel   Literally, the Women's Department; the Party organization founded in 1919 that promoted women's emancipation; abolished 1930.

zhensovety   Literally, women's soviets; organizations established in the late 1950s at the local and regional level to promote women's involvement in civic projects and raise their productivity at work.

NOTES ON BIBLIOGRAPHY

Those wishing to learn more about the history of Soviet women can choose from a wealth of materials. What follows here is a very brief introduction to the rapidly growing bibliography.

SCHOLARLY STUDIES

Among scholarly works the most comprehensive is Gail Warshofsky Lapidus' *Women in Soviet Society* (Berkeley, 1978). Lapidus concentrates on the development and evolution of government policies toward women and on the ways in which these changed the position of women in Soviet society. Mary Buckley's *Women and Ideology in the Soviet Union* (Ann Arbor, 1989) complements Lapidus' study and is especially illuminating in discussing the period after 1953.

The shifting position of women in the economic life of the U.S.S.R. and particularly in the paid labor force has been the subject of several books as well as numerous articles. The foundation was laid by Norton Dodge in his *Women in the Soviet Economy* (Baltimore, 1966). Dodge conducted exhaustive research into all aspects of women's work, both waged labor and the double shift. The result is a book rich in statistics about and analysis of postwar developments. Michael Paul Sacks in *Women's Work in Soviet Russia: Continuity in the Midst of Change* (New York, 1976) and Martin McAuley in *Women's Work and Wages in the U.S.S.R.* (London, 1981) then extended the analysis back to 1917 and forward into the 1970s. Finally, Susan Bridger in *Women in the Soviet Countryside* (Cambridge, 1987) provides a detailed examination of peasant women's work (concentrating on the 1960s and 1970s) and like Sacks, McAuley, and Dodge, studies as well women's family lives, education, and values.

There are two monographs on developments in the 1920s and 1930s. Gregory Massell wrote a substantive analysis of the Zhenotdel's effort to emancipate Central-Asian women: *The Surrogate Proletariat: Moslem Women and Revolutionary Strategies in Soviet Central Asia, 1919–1929* (Princeton, 1974). Wendy

Goldman has looked at developments in family life in *The Withering Away and Resurrection of the Soviet Family, 1917–1936* (Cambridge, 1993).

Those wishing to explore the origins of the Bolshevik program of women's emancipation, as well as the intelligentsia's discussion of the woman question in the nineteenth century, should consult Richard Stites' *The Women's Liberation Movement in Russia: Feminism, Nihilism, and Bolshevism,* 2d ed. (Princeton, 1991).

Other aspects of Soviet women's history are best explored by working through the articles that have been published. There are so many of these that they cannot all be mentioned; references to them can be found in indices of social-science periodicals. Several collections of articles dealing with Soviet women's history do warrant discussion here, however.

One of the most useful is *Promissory Notes: Women in the Transition to Socialism,* edited by Sonia Kruks, Rayna Rapp, and Marilyn B. Young (New York, 1989). This substantial collection of essays on women and Stalinist-style socialism around the globe, from the Soviet Union to China, illuminates the Soviet case in a cross-cultural perspective.

Two other collections set the experience of Soviet women in historical perspective. They are *Russia's Women: Accommodation, Resistance, Transformation,* edited by Barbara Evans Clements, Barbara Alpern Engel, and Christine D. Worobec (Berkeley, 1991); and *Russian Peasant Women,* edited by Beatrice Farnsworth and Lynne Viola (New York, 1992). Each consists of articles that analyze various aspects of women's history in the tsarist and Soviet periods, but both pay particular attention to women's work and reproductive lives, as well as to social values and customs.

There are also useful collections of articles available on recent developments. *Soviet Sisterhood,* edited by Barbara Holland (Bloomington, 1985), contains essays that analyze women's situation during the Brezhnev years. *Women and Perestroika,* edited by Mary Buckley (Cambridge, 1992), performs a similar service for the Gorbachev period.

As yet, few biographies of prominent Soviet women have been written by Western scholars. Alexandra Kollontai has received the greatest attention, being the subject of three books: Barbara Evans Clements, *Bolshevik Feminist* (Bloomington, 1979); Beatrice

Farnsworth, *Alexandra Kollontai: Socialism, Feminism, and the Bolshevik Revolution* (Stanford, 1980); and Cathy Porter, *Alexandra Kollontai* (London, 1978). Robert McNeal wrote a sympathetic portrait of Nadezhda Krupskaia, *Bride of the Revolution: Krupskaya and Lenin* (Ann Arbor, 1972). And R. C. Elwood has recently published a thoroughly researched study, *Inessa Armand, Revolutionary and Feminist* (Cambridge, 1992).

Biographies of the great female writers of twentieth-century Russian literature are also available. Simon Karlinsky wrote a highly regarded biography of the poet Marina Tsvetaeva, *Marina Tsvetaeva, the Woman, her World, and her Poetry* (Cambridge, 1986). Anna Akhmatova is the subject of Amanda Haight's *Anna Akhmatova: A Poetic Pilgrimage* (New York, 1976).

PRIMARY WORKS

Those wishing to read what Soviet women themselves have written may be surprised to learn that a great many works have been translated into English, so many in fact that this essay can only discuss a fraction of them.

Several of the greatest figures in Russian literature in the twentieth century were women. The poetry of Anna Akhmatova and Marina Tsvetaeva is available in a variety of editions. Evgenia Ginzburg's two-volume memoir of her imprisonment in the GULAG in the 1930s and 1940s, *Into the Whirlwind* (New York, 1967), and *Within the Whirlwind* (New York, 1981) is a literary masterpiece, as well as one of the great studies of concentration-camp life. Other powerful memoirs of the Stalin years are Nadezhda Mandelshtam's *Hope Against Hope* (New York, 1970) and *Hope Abandoned* (New York, 1974).

The work of today's Soviet female writers can also teach the outsider a great deal about women's lives and about Soviet society. *Balancing Acts*, edited by Helena Goscilo (Bloomington, 1989), is a rich collection of engaging and enlightening short stories. Goscilo has also published stories by Polish and Russian writers in *Russian and Polish Women's Fiction* (Knoxville, 1985). Perhaps the best known short story by a Soviet woman is Natalia Baranskaia's "A Week Like Any Other Week." This touching portrayal of the double shift is available in English (*Massachusetts Review* 15 [Autumn 1974]: 657–703).

Nonfictional portraits of Soviet women have been published both by outside observers (most commonly journalists) and by Soviet citizens themselves. The best deal with women in the Brezhnev and Gorbachev periods. Among the journalists, the most sensitive to women is Elizabeth Pond's *From the Yaroslavsky Station*, 3d ed. (New York, 1988). Her work is nicely complemented by an interesting collection of interviews with Soviet women published by Swedish scholars Carola Hansson and Karin Liden, *Moscow Women* (New York, 1983). Gail Warshofsky Lapidus edited a collection of articles by Soviet social scientists on women, *Women, Work, and Family in the Soviet Union* (Armonk, N.Y., 1982). And finally, the samizdat feminist journal *Almanac: Woman and Russia* is available in translation as *Women and Russia: Feminist Writings from the Soviet Union*, edited by Tatyana Mamonova (Boston, 1984).

STATISTICS

The statistics cited in the text come from the following sources:

Chapter 2

Barbara Evans Clements, "Baba and Bolshevik: Russian Women and Revolutionary Change," *Soviet Union*, 12, pt. 2 (1985): 165–66; Rose Glickman, *Russian Factory Women: Workplace and Society, 1880–1914* (Berkeley, 1984); R. E. Johnson, "Family Life in Moscow During NEP," in *Russia in the Era of NEP: Explorations in Soviet Society and Culture* (Bloomington, 1991), 109; Diane Koenker, "Urbanization and Deurbanization in the Russian Revolution and Civil War," *Party, State, and Society in the Russian Civil War*, eds. Diane P. Koenker, William G. Rosenberg, and Ronald Grigor Suny (Bloomington, 1989), 81; Moshe Lewin, *The Making of the Soviet System* (New York, 1985); Alfred G. Meyer, "The Impact of World War I on Russian Women's Lives," *Russia's Women: Accommodation, Resistance, Transformation*, ed. Barbara Evans Clements, Barbara Alpern Engel, and Christine Worobec (Berkeley, 1991), 214, 213; Maureen Perrie, "The Social Composition and Structure of the Socialist-Revolutionary Party before 1917," *Soviet Studies* 24 (1972): 235.

Chapter 3

Susan Bridger, *Women in the Soviet Countryside* (New York, 1987); P. M. Chirkov, *Reshenie zhenskogo voprosa v SSSR (1917–1937)* (Moscow, 1978); F. M. Knuniants-Rizel', "Docheri partii," *Uchastnitsy velikogo sozidanie* (Moscow, 1962), 14–16; *Kommunistka*, no. 9 (1927): 28, 30, no. 10 (1927): 61, 63, 64, 67; Roberta Manning, "Women in the Soviet Countryside on the Eve of World War II," *Russian Peasant Women,* ed. Beatrice Farnsworth and Lynn Viola (New York, 1992), 220; Michael Paul Sacks, *Women's Work in Soviet Russia: Continuity in the Midst of Change* (New York, 1976); E. Smitten, "Zhenshchiny v R.K.P.," *Kommunistka*, no. 1–2 (1923): 30; Tsentral'noe statisticheskoe upravlenie, *Statisticheskii spravochnik SSSR za 1928 g.* (Moscow, 1929); *Zhenshchiny SSSR: Statisticheskii sbornik* (Moscow, 1975).

Chapter 4

John Barber and Mark Harrison, *The Soviet Home Front, 1941–1945* (London, 1991); K. Jean Cottam, "Soviet Women in Combat in World War II: The Ground Forces and the Navy," *International Journal of Women's Studies* 3, no. 4 (1980): 345–57; K. Jean Cottam, "Soviet Women in Combat in World War II: The Rear Services, Resistance Behind Enemy Lines and Military Political Workers," *International Journal of Women's Studies* 3 (1980): 363–78; Kenneth D. Slepyan, "Soviet Partisans: Women and the Concept of *Vsenarodnaia voina*," paper presented at the Midwest Slavic Conference, May 2, 1993.

Chapter 5

Susan Bridger, *Women in the Soviet Countryside: Women's Roles in Rural Development in the Soviet Union* (Cambridge, 1987); Gail Warshofsky Lapidus, ed., *Women, Work, and Family in the Soviet Union* (Berkeley, 1982); *Soviet Sisterhood*, ed. Barbara Holland (Bloomington, 1985); *The World's Women: Trends and Statistics* (New York, 1991); *Zhenshchiny SSSR: Statisticheskii sbornik* (Moscow, 1975).

Chapter 6

Mary Buckley, ed., *Perestroika and Soviet Women* (Cambridge, 1992).

INDEX

Illustration Credits:

Pages x, xi. Russian peasant women in a farmstead courtyard in central Russia, circa 1910. Library of Congress

Page 8. Sofia Perovskaia, in a sketch by P. IA. Piasetskii made at the time of her trial in 1881. From *Illiustrirovannaia istoriia SSSR* (Moscow 1977)

Page 35. Alexandra Kollontai. From A. Kollontai, *Is moei zhizni i raboty*, ed. I. M. Dazhina (Moscow 1974)

Page 67. Praskovia Angelina. From Arkadii Slavutskii, *Praskovia Angelina* (Moscow 1960)

Page 108. Anna Akhmatova. Library of Congress

Page 131. Valentina Tereshkova. Photograph by Vera Zhiharenko. Tass/Sovfoto

Page 137. The village doctor. Photograph by Alexander Uzlyan

Page 141. Sofia Ivanovna Iurkova. Photograph courtesy of William Husband

All illustrations used with permission except where unable to locate artist.

Daughters of Revolution: A History of Women in the U.S.S.R.
Sponsoring editor and copy editor, Maureen Hewitt
Production editor, Lucy Herz
Field editor, Jura Avizienis
Proofreader, Carolee Lipsey
Typesetter, Bruce Leckie
Printer, McNaughton & Gunn, Inc.
Cartographer, James Bier
Book designer, Roger Eggers

About the Author: Barbara Evans Clements, Professor of History at the University of Akron, teaches Russian history and women's history. In addition to having written *Daughters of Revolution: A History of Women in the U.S.S.R.* for the European History Series, she is author of *Bolshevik Feminist: The Life of Alexandra Kollontai,* and co-editor of *Russia's Women: Accommodation, Resistance, Transformation.*